INSTRUCTOR'S MANUAL

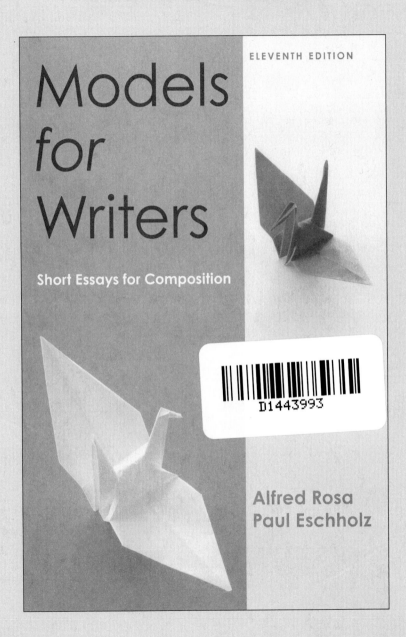

ELEVENTH EDITION

Models
for
Writers

Short Essays for Composition

Alfred Rosa
Paul Eschholz

D1443993

Instructor's Manual
for

Models
for
Writers

Short Essays for Composition

ELEVENTH EDITION

Alfred Rosa
Paul Eschholz

Prepared by
Sarah Federman

BEDFORD/ST. MARTIN'S
Boston ◆ *New York*

Manufactured in the United States of America.

6 5 4 3 2
f e d c b a

For information, write: Bedford/St. Martin's, 75 Arlington Street, Boston, MA
02116   (617-399-4000)

ISBN: 978-0-312-55218-3

Preface

The purpose of this *Instructor's Manual* is to help you use *Models for Writers* with the greatest effectiveness. We therefore provide an analysis and key discussion points for each selection in the book. In these sections of the manual, labeled *Essay Analysis and Discussion*, we share our experiences in teaching the essays: what to stress, what to explain, what to ask about, and what to expect in general from discussions. A typical analysis might do one or more of the following:

- Explore one or more content issues
- Point out stylistic features
- Suggest classroom activities that reinforce rhetorical strategies
- Suggest one or more other essays in the text that might be usefully taught in conjunction with the present one
- Explain where students are likely to have difficulty understanding either content or rhetorical techniques

In addition, in the section *Questions for Study and Discussion* we provide suggested responses to the questions following each selection in *Models for Writers*. Our intent is to save you time, not dictate answers. On occasion, you may disagree with our interpretation or emphasis, but we trust that the suggested responses will at least be useful as starting points. Your own experience with each essay will be invaluable, as will common sense about what will challenge and engage your students. Also included in this manual are suggested answers for the *Thinking Critically about This Reading* exercises and detailed discussions of what you might expect from each of the *Classroom Activities*.

The essays in *Models for Writers* are grouped into 21 chapters, each devoted to a separate rhetorical topic. Chapters 3 through 10 focus on specific elements of essays: thesis, unity, organization, beginnings and endings, paragraphs, transitions, effective sentences, and writing with sources. Chapters 11 and 12 concern some uses and effects of language: diction and tone, and figurative language. Finally, Chapters 13 through 21 explore types of essays: illustration, narration, description, process analysis, definition, division and classification, comparison and contrast, cause and effect, and argument.

The arrangement of the chapters suggests a logical teaching sequence, beginning with the elements of an essay, proceeding through the language of an essay, and then covering the types of essays. An alternative teaching strategy is to structure your course according to the types of essays, teaching other chapters as necessary or having students use them for reference. Finally, because each chapter is self-contained, you can design your own teaching sequence, omitting or emphasizing particular chapters according to the special needs of your class.

To help you use *Models for Writers* effectively, we would like to call your attention to the following special features.

Introductory Section on Reading and Writing Well. In Chapter 1, "The Writing Process," students learn useful questions to ask themselves as they undertake the writing process. By showing a student's essay in progress, beginning with developing an idea for an essay and ending in a final draft, the chapter allows students to see the writing process step by step.

In Chapter 2, "From Reading to Writing," students learn how to become active readers. Annotated examples help students understand the best ways to prepare themselves to read a selection, read a selection for the first time, reread the selection, annotate the text with marginal notes, and analyze the text by asking questions. The chapter concludes with a discussion of how one uses reading in the writing process. Here we include four annotated student essays to illustrate four types of essays—narrative, response, reflective, and analytical—that students typically write in college. In addition, the sample papers give students a good idea of the length and quality of writing they should be striving to produce. We therefore suggest that you assign the first two chapters early in the course and that you spend as much time as possible discussing the four student papers and their salient features.

Chapter Introductions. Before reading the essays in a particular chapter, students should read that chapter's introduction. There they will find an explanation of the rhetorical principle under consideration and a discussion of how it can be used. The information in the introductions will also help students answer the questions and complete the writing assignments that accompany each selection.

Reflecting on What You Know. Preceding each reading are prereading activities that prompt students to explore their own ideas and experiences regarding the issues presented in the reading.

Critical Thinking Questions. Each selection is followed by a prompt that encourages students to think critically about their reading by exploring—in discussion or in writing—the author's meaning and assumptions as well as the broader implications of the selection.

Questions for Study and Discussion. The study questions for each selection focus on its content, its author's purpose, and the rhetorical principle used to achieve that purpose. Some questions require brief answers; others are intended to stimulate class discussion. Because students' knowledge of rhetorical techniques and patterns will increase as the course proceeds, we have included for each essay one or more questions about rhetorical elements other than the one highlighted in the particular essay.

Classroom Activities. These brief exercises (requiring fifteen to twenty minutes in most cases) enable students to work with each rhetorical element, technique, or pattern while in the classroom, often in groups. The activities included here will help students develop thesis statements, organize sentences within paragraphs, use strong action verbs, work with connotation and denotation, use figurative language, use examples to document a generalization, use facts effectively, work with outlines for comparison and contrast, test cause-and-effect relationships, classify on the basis of distinctive characteristics, and build argumentative evidence. Frequently, these activities require students to engage in critical thinking and problem solving. We have used all these activities in our own writing classes, and our students have found them helpful.

Suggested Writing Assignments. At least two writing assignments accompany each essay in the textbook. They offer students the opportunity to apply the rhetorical principle at hand. Often these assignments are also related to the content of the essays. If you prefer not to assign all the readings, most can be assigned independently.

Visual Writing Prompts. Five new advertisements in the argument chapter encourage students to analyze the visual texts they see every day.

Brief Guide to Writing a Research Paper. A new Chapter 22 on writing a research paper covers such essential topics as establishing a realistic schedule; finding, evaluating, and synthesizing print and online sources; taking notes; and developing a working bibliography. Also provided are models for using the most current Modern Language Association documentation style, including in-text citations and lists of works cited, and a new annotated student research paper.

Glossary of Useful Terms. The glossary, located at the end of the book, provides students with concise definitions of terms useful for discussing the readings and their own writing. Wherever we have believed that information in the glossary might assist students in answering a study question, we have placed a cross reference to the appropriate glossary entry next to the question.

Thematic Contents. If a particular essay evokes strong student response, this alternative table of contents makes it easier for you to choose thematically related pieces in other sections of *Models for Writers*. Nearly all the readings are entered under at least one subject heading, and many appear under two or three. Admittedly, some of these classifications may seem a bit arbitrary, but we believe that none are misfits. Beyond calling attention to the content of individual essays, this listing also allows you to point out different rhetorical approaches to common themes.

Online Reading Quizzes. The *Models for Writers* Companion Web site (bedfordstmartins.com/models) features an online reading quiz for each selection.

We are very much interested in hearing from anyone who has constructive ideas about the content or use of either *Models for Writers* or this manual. We can be reached at the Department of English, 400 Old Mill, University of Vermont, Burlington, VT 05405.

Alfred Rosa
Paul Eschholz
Sarah Federman

v

Contents

Crime: What Constitutes an Effective Punishment?

Advertising: How Does it Affect Our Lives?

Torture: Are We For or Against It?

CHAPTER 3 **Thesis**

The Most Important Day (p. 84)
■ **Helen Keller**

Essay Analysis and Discussion

The first paragraph of this essay, although short, is vital to establishing focus and direction for the paragraphs that follow. The first sentence states the thesis, but without the two sentences following it, the essay would lose the unity Keller has achieved. To get students to see the connection between the thesis statement and the opening paragraph as a whole, and their relation to the rest of the essay, have them consider what each of the first three sentences accomplishes in regard to the other paragraphs. It may help to look at the stages of Keller's narration (as they are outlined in study question 6) to see if there is a correlation between those stages and the three sentences in the opening paragraph. The students' analysis should reveal that although the thesis statement focuses on a particular day, the essay can include discussion of other days and other events and still remain unified because of the context established by the entire first paragraph.

Thinking Critically about This Reading

The light Keller refers to is the ability to communicate through language. Draw students' attention to Keller's metaphor at the beginning of paragraph 3 describing the ship lost at night in the fog and to Keller's statement in paragraph 7 that "the living word awakened my soul, gave it light, hope, joy, set it free!"

Questions for Study and Discussion

1. Keller's thesis is the first sentence of the essay. Keller answers the question "What is the most important day in my life and why?" This question focuses Keller on a specific period in her life, that time when Anne Mansfield Sullivan opened up the world of words to her, which, in turn, let her think and communicate with others. Keller's thesis answers the first part of the question, and her narrative explains the importance of that day.
2. Keller's purpose is to *tell* why the day that Anne Sullivan came to her was the most important day in her life.
3. For several weeks before Anne Sullivan arrived, Keller was angry and bitter. When that passed she fell into a "deep languor" (2). She compared the feeling to being a ship in a fog of darkness groping its way to shore.

1

4. Every new name gave birth to a new thought. Words would "make the world blossom for me" (9).

5. Keller understood the connection between words and the things they describe one day, after many such days, when her teacher placed one of Keller's hands under running water while she spelled the word *water* in the other. "Suddenly I felt a misty consciousness as of something forgotten—a thrill of returning thought; and somehow the mystery of language was revealed to me" (7).

6. On the first day, she meets Anne Sullivan and they embrace. On the next day, Anne Sullivan gives her a doll and spells the word *doll* on her hand until Keller is able to imitate the spelling. Several weeks later, Anne again tries to make the connection for Keller between objects and words (e.g., *mug* and *water* and *doll*) and is finally able to accomplish this connection at the well-house with the word *water* and the water itself.

Classroom Activity Using Thesis

Some questions that our students suggested include the following:

1. How serious is our campus wastepaper problem?
2. How much of our paper waste is currently being recycled?
3. How can our wastepaper be effectively used?
4. What is made from recycled paper?
5. What are the problems of collecting wastepaper on campus?
6. Is recycling paper waste an economic or an environmental issue, or both?
7. Does the campus newspaper use recycled newsprint?
8. What recycled paper products are currently being used on campus?
9. If we do not recycle wastepaper on campus, what will be the effect on our environment?
10. What other items, if any, are being recycled on campus?

Your students will come up with questions of their own, questions that perhaps focus on particular situations on your campus. Ask students to discuss what information is needed and where they would be likely to obtain that information to answer each of the questions here on recycling.

Be Specific (p. 90)
■ Natalie Goldberg

Essay Analysis and Discussion

Goldberg's message in this essay is simple and to the point: "Be specific." We all recognize when a writer is specific; the writing seems to come alive, to jump off the page, to create vivid and memorable pictures in the mind of the reader. But beginning writers have difficulty being specific, using telling details. Goldberg offers some direct advice for students to start with: Give people and things names and provide a specific context (month, day, moment, etc.) for the situation about which you are writing. Not only does Goldberg give writers advice about being specific, she also demonstrates that advice in her own writing, by effectively including many names, details, and examples in her essay. Yet, when she tries to explain why specificity is a positive virtue, the poetic and mystical reasons that she provides, ironically, seem vague or hard to grasp exactly. She says that using a flower's name "penetrates more deeply into the beingness of that flower" (paragraph 1) and allows us to penetrate "more deeply into the present and being there." (paragraph 5). In her concluding paragraphs, Goldberg asks readers to "learn the names of all the other group members" and to learn "the names of everything: birds, cheese, tractors, cars, buildings." As class exercises, have students learn each other's names, and ask the class to generate lists of names for items in each of the five general categories she suggests.

Thinking Critically about This Reading

By being specific about what we call things, we can be sure to refer to those things correctly. Just as it is inaccurate to call Joe by the name of George, so it is with things. Goldberg says writers should refer to things by their specific names because "[w]hen we know the name of something . . . [i]t takes the blur out of our mind; it connects us to the earth" (paragraph 3).

Questions for Study and Discussion

1. Goldberg practices what she preaches in this essay. She is careful to "be specific." She "give[s] things the dignity of their names," and she set out to learn the names of everything, concentrating first on "the names of plants and flowers in my environment."

2. The lists help define the word *specific* because each list is made up of particular members of a general category. The lists forcefully show that names do, in fact, convey precise images; each name on the list removes a particular object from its category by bringing to mind a picture of that object in a setting furnished by the reader's imagination.

3. Goldberg follows the first Williams quotation by restating what he says, which allows her to extrapolate beyond his description of the daisy, linking his words to her main argument for specificity.

4. Goldberg uses the Blake quotation to reinforce her argument that specificity gives a greater sense of real life.

5. Goldberg uses Williams and Blake to reinforce her main argument, but also as examples of specificity in action.

6. According to Goldberg's example (addressing a person by her name rather than by "girl"), people—and by extension, things—are dignified when they

are recognized by name as specific individuals instead of as members of a general class. "Integrity" implies uniqueness, wholeness, and self-worth.

7. Goldberg addresses writers. In paragraph 4, she quotes William Carlos Williams: "Write what's in front of your nose." She mentions writing groups (6) and gives advice to "a writer" (7).

Classroom Activity Using Thesis

Students' answers will vary. Here are some sample or possible answers.

A *general* name for a writing instrument: pen.
A *more general* name for a sandwich: lunch food.
A *general name* for an American: Native American.
A *more specific* name for a dictionary: *American Heritage Dictionary*.
A *more specific* name for a technical high school: The John D. O'Bryant School of Mathematics and Science.
A *more specific* name for a gel capsule: Nordic Naturals Omega 3 Fish Gelatin Caps

Anxiety: Challenge by Another Name (p. 94)
■ **James Lincoln Collier**

Essay Analysis and Discussion

Collier arranges his essay chronologically, from his youth to the present, to demonstrate his thesis that we can learn to overcome the stultifying effects of anxiety. At each major decision in his life, he uses examples from philosophy, psychology, and other people's lives to illustrate and strengthen his argument. The examples he chooses are common enough that the reader can sympathize with and relate to the author's point of view. At three different points, Collier also punctuates the essay with his rule and its corollaries, the conclusions he has drawn about anxiety and its relationship to learning. Ask students to think about some of the rules they have learned for themselves. Then ask them to describe, using examples, how these rules might have universal application. Remind them to use examples of situations that are easily identified by the other students in the class. They might try writing about lessons they learned over time as well as those they learned quickly after one hapless episode. How would the arrangement of material differ in that case?

Thinking Critically about This Reading

Collier's own experiences (see study question 3) echo his statement in paragraph 9 that "it seems to be a rule of life that you can't advance without getting that old, familiar, jittery feeling" and support the similar observation made by

Kierkegaard. Ask students whether their experiences have led them to the same conclusions as Collier and Kierkegaard.

Questions for Study and Discussion

1. Collier states his thesis in paragraph 20: "The point is that the new, the different, is almost by definition scary. But each time you try something, you learn, and as the learning piles up, the world opens to you." Students will explain their own experiences with Collier's thesis.
2. Collier explains extinction in paragraph 14.
3. Collier came up with his basic rule for himself after turning down an offer to work in Argentina one summer. He developed his first corollary as a result of reflecting on what he went through while interviewing famous people. He developed his second corollary as a result of his hesitating to accept a three-month assignment to work in Europe. By sharing the three experiences that led him to develop his basic rule and the two corollaries, Collier makes it easy for readers to accept his thesis. By the time readers reach paragraph 20, they are already familiar with the life situations that gave Collier his insight and understanding.
4. Collier means to demonstrate, based on his own experience, that we can overcome anxiety and in so doing can live a richer, fuller life.
5. These paragraphs contrast with the first paragraph in Collier's essay to show that over time he has learned to overcome the kind of anxiety that kept him "safe" at home when he was a young adult.

Classroom Activity Using Thesis

Sentences 1, 2, and 4 identify the topic and make an assertion about that topic that the writer must document in the body of the essay. Sentences 3 and 5, however, are weak as thesis statements; both sentences are too general and opinionated. By way of discussion, have students talk about what they would expect to read in an essay about each topic. Students' expectations for sentences 1, 2, and 4 should be clearer than their expectations for sentences 3 and 5.

CHAPTER 4 Unity

My Favorite Teacher (p. 103)
■ Thomas L. Friedman

Essay Analysis and Discussion

Friedman's description of Hattie Steinberg is built on examples that show the kind of influence she had on her students. As a class activity to demonstrate

5

the role that examples can play in describing an individual, have students list important high school experiences involving teachers, good or bad. When you have a sufficient number of examples, discuss what each reveals about the teacher-student dynamic and, based on the example, have your students draw a descriptive conclusion about the teacher involved. After completing this process for all the examples, you should have a list of experiences and conclusions that demonstrates the relationship between general observations and specific illustrations.

Thinking Critically about This Reading

Students may have varying interpretations of what Friedman means by this statement. Many of their responses will probably mention that the Internet provides information, but it does nor help the user to develop character when it comes to applying that information.

Questions for Study and Discussion

1. Friedman's examples point out key aspects of his own career in journalism, thereby establishing the important role Hattie Steinberg has played in his life. His interview with an advertising executive for his high school paper, during which the advertising executive used a four-letter word that Friedman and Steinberg decided to print, taught Friedman about the consequences of one's behavior. His description of his first published story for the school paper, for which he covered a lecture by and then interviewed Ariel Sharon, indicates the direction his career followed, focusing on issues in the Middle East. The *New York Times* was delivered every morning to Room 313. The paper exerted an enormous influence over Friedman's approach to journalism, beginning the professional path that led him from being Steinberg's student to a successful columnist for the *Times*. Finally, Friedman's example about the "dot-com-Internet-globalization bubble" that burst impresses upon readers the real secret to success that Steinberg passed on to him: fundamentals.

2. At the end of paragraph 10, Friedman presents characteristics that represent Steinberg's understanding of fundamentals: reading; writing; arithmetic; church, synagogue, and mosque; the rule of law; and good governance. Friedman uses this series of items to illustrate how what Steinberg taught about journalism applied to the larger concerns of life as well.

3. Examples of short sentences in Friedman's essay include the following:
   "She wanted to teach us about consequences." (3)
   "Competition was fierce." (4)
   "His name was Ariel Sharon. First story I ever got published." (4)
   "She was a woman of clarity in an age of uncertainty." (5)
   "These fundamentals cannot be downloaded." (11)

In each case, the short sentence emphasizes the key point developed in the paragraph in which it appears. Students' opinions about how the sentences affect them as readers may vary, but most will probably acknowledge the way the sentences contribute to the main ideas presented throughout the essay or the manner in which they create a sense of rhythm and fluency in the prose by varying sentence length and structure.

4. Friedman's repeated references to Room 313 reflect the deep impression that the activities within that room made on him and the amount of time he spent there during high school. Now when he thinks of his experiences with Hattie Steinberg, he thinks of Room 313.

5. Students' opinions about which examples stand out for them and why Friedman chose those examples may vary. Whichever they select, however, the general idea conveyed should reflect Friedman's emphasis on Steinberg's stern but principled and committed behavior toward her students.

6. Friedman believes that in the rush to make a lot of money quickly, the dot-coms "forgot the fundamentals of how you build a profitable company." Students may or may not agree with Friedman's statement.

Classroom Activity Using Unity

The following sentences disrupt the unity of the essay:

> "Most of the students lived in an impoverished neighborhood that had only one park for several thousand residents." (2)
> "Mr. Norant was known to students as Twiggy Iggy because of his tall, thin frame." (2)
> "A cheerleader in college, Ms. Peña got her B.A. in recreation science before getting her masters in education." (3)

Although the descriptions are interesting and give color to the story, they are irrelevant to the point and distracting.

My Name (p. 109)
■ Sandra Cisneros

Essay Analysis and Discussion

Cisneros's essay is at once simple and challenging. Despite its brevity, it should yield several excellent discussion topics. First, its unity may not be apparent to many students, especially in paragraph 3. Cisneros's great-grandmother is vital to the discussion of her name, however, because of the obvious connection they have, not just in their given names but in their personalities. Students should understand the irony that two such strong-willed women should be named "hope." Also discuss why Cisneros presents her name so late in her essay. What does the reader think while reading the essay before Cisneros states her name? How does having to wait to consider why the name is like the number nine or a muddy color make the similes in the first paragraph more effective? Finally, students should enjoy the idea of choosing a new name. What does Zeze the X communicate to them about Cisneros?

Thinking Critically about This Reading

Cisneros states that Mexicans "don't like their women strong" (paragraph 2). Before she married, Cisneros's great-grandmother was "a wild horse of a woman" (3); after she married, she became tame and docile and let the world pass her by. Cisneros does not want to lose herself the way her great-grandmother did after she married.

Questions for Study and Discussion

1. Cisneros's thesis is that she has inherited her grandmother's name, with all its associations, but she does not want to be trapped by it. She states the thesis at the end of paragraph 4.
2. Cisneros's essay is unified in that each paragraph is logically related to her thesis. There are no digressions, and there is no unrelated discussion or information. In the first paragraph, she presents the meaning and associations of her name. In paragraphs 2 through 4, she presents the family history of her name and of her identification with the personality of her great-grandmother, if not with her ultimate situation. In paragraph 5, she establishes how she is unable to escape her name. In paragraph 6, she explains just how far she would go to escape it.
3. The name *Esperanza* is part of a culture that does not encourage strength in women. Using her name as the subject, Cisneros presents her heritage of cultural restrictions and her overwhelming desire to escape them.
4. The similes are open to interpretation, but students should demonstrate that some thought went into their answers. Most students, after having read the essay, will probably say that the similes give the impression that the narrator holds a negative opinion of the name, but other interpretations may be more complex.
5. Cisneros's tone is angry and defiant. She establishes it best in paragraph 2, where she attacks the Chinese for their view of women that parallels the Hispanic one. She also says bluntly that she will not be at all content with her great-grandmother's role in life. The tone helps her convey her desire to escape the associations that her name carries with it.
6. This question is open to various interpretations, but Cisneros involves the reader by presenting intriguing similes and an intriguing personality associated with her name without revealing what the name is. The reader wonders what name is like a muddy color or the number nine, and by the

time it is revealed, the reader is interested and aware of Cisneros's contempt for what her name implies.

7. Again, this question is open to interpretation. Most students should pick up on it being unusual, dramatic, and hard-edged.

Classroom Activity Using Unity

Paragraph 2, while important, is out of place in the essay. The essay is how to build a fire, not about safe fire methods. The point about the chimney is vital, but it is not related to the process the author seeks to describe.

The Meanings of a Word (p. 113)
■ Gloria Naylor

Essay Analysis and Discussion

In her essay, Naylor uses illustration to argue that there are two different definitions of the word *nigger*, depending on who is using it and to what purpose. In so doing, Naylor makes the larger point that all language is similarly subject to interpretation and change depending on the context. Readers will notice that Naylor concentrates most of her essay on illustrating the lesser-known meaning of the word *nigger* as it is used in African American culture. This imbalance is based on Naylor's assumption that most of her readers will be familiar with the racist connotation of the word as it is used in the white culture. Students can choose another word that has both a familiar and a lesser-known meaning; then, using Naylor's essay as a guide, they can illustrate the ways in which the understanding of that word changes from culture to culture or from speaker to speaker.

Thinking Critically about This Reading

Naylor means that words in and of themselves are powerless. Not until a majority of people agree on the meaning of a word is it imbued with significance and power. In the larger white community, the word *nigger* has a very strong and specific racist meaning; in the smaller African American community, however, the word—when used by and among other African Americans—is a term of familiarity. The racist meaning of the word trumps its other meanings because more people recognize the power of its negative connotations.

Questions for Study and Discussion

1. The subject of Naylor's opening two paragraphs is language. Although Naylor has the greatest respect for the written word, she considers the spoken word more powerful, coming at the instant of a thought and being

9

expressed in the full dynamic interplay of all the senses. She points out that words are simply arbitrary symbols that derive their meaning from the consensus of people who use them. She develops this thesis in the remainder of her essay with a series of examples.

2. Naylor best defines the word *nigger* in its role as a racial slur in paragraph 14: "a word that whites used to signify worthlessness or degradation." *Nigger* as used by African Americans is best expressed in the same paragraph: "Gathering there together, they transformed *nigger* to signify the varied and complex human beings they knew themselves to be."

3. Naylor means simply that the word *nigger* was used in her family in a context of love, admiration, and affection that allowed it to dwell there comfortably and unnoticed. In her third-grade class, she heard it expressed in a hostile context for an altogether different purpose—as an insult. In other words, it was not the same word she had heard all her life, and so she was hearing it for the first time.

4. Naylor includes details of her family's history, its structure, the neighborhood in which they all lived, the activities they enjoyed, the ways they earned their livings, and the substance of their conversations as a means of establishing the context in which their use of the word *nigger* arose. The little she offers in the way of a definition of the word *nigger* as used by the white community is disquieting to any reader who notices the omission and so is jolted to an awareness of not needing to be told what the word means.

5. Naylor could hardly have been faulted had she used an angry tone to describe the different meanings of the word *nigger*, but she has chosen to use a level, objective tone, as if she were standing back casting a cool, refined glance at the phenomenon that has hurt so many of her people. In paragraph 3, when she recounts the moment she first heard the word *nigger* as a slur, Naylor describes the event rather matter-of-factly: "I remember the first time I heard the word *nigger*. . . . Had he called me a nymphomaniac or a necrophiliac, I couldn't have been more puzzled." Throughout her essay she analyzes the meaning of the word *nigger* as an anthropologist might, using the impartiality of the scientific method. Not until her final sentence does Naylor reveal the sadness and fatigue that we can assume came after who knows how long an effort to assimilate her initial feelings of confusion, shock, anger, and betrayal.

6. Naylor's last sentence is effective for reminding the reader once again that "in America" the primary use of the word *nigger* will be as a racial slur and is one that most readers do not have to sit on their mothers' laps to have explained.

Classroom Activity Using Unity

This activity can be enhanced if students then provide another paragraph to classmates. Small groups of four students work best. Having students look at one another's writing also will help them overcome shyness associated with having someone else review one's writing. Ultimately, it also encourages students to look to their peers, not just teachers, for input. This collaboration is an invaluable skill in the workplace.

CHAPTER 5 **Organization**

A View from the Bridge (p. 124)
■ Cherokee Paul McDonald

Essay Analysis and Discussion

McDonald's essay is remarkable not only for the story he tells but also for the vivid description he uses. He organizes his narration chronologically and lets his story unfold through the use of dialogue between the narrator (presumably McDonald himself) and the young boy fishing. This dialogue enables McDonald to show us that the child is blind instead of telling us. Interestingly, the events that McDonald recounts occur within a half hour. Finally, take the opportunity this essay offers to discuss with your students what it means to "see." How, for example, are the narrator and the boy using the word "see" in paragraphs 42 and 43?

Thinking Critically about This Reading

The narrator is both acknowledging the boy's thanks and reciprocating them. As he describes the tarpon carefully to please the boy, the narrator comes to his own renewed sense of wonder and appreciation for the beauty of the fish.

Questions for Study and Discussion

1. McDonald has organized his essay chronologically. The essay recounts an incident that took place in perhaps thirty minutes, or certainly no more than an hour.

2. The boy wore "wrap-around sunglasses" (paragraph 3). He was "fumbling" with his rod and reel (4), he could not see the shrimp by his foot (10), his fingers "felt for the drag setting" (16), he thought he had lost the fish when the line went slack (20), and he asked the narrator to tell him what the fish looked like (29). The narrator does not realize that the boy is blind because he is preoccupied with his jogging and because the kid is a competent fisherman whose behavior does not arouse suspicion.

3. The narrator seeks to use words and phrases that are familiar to a child. He also looks for words that appeal to a sense other than sight. (For example, he starts to say that the fish is three feet long but then changes to the

11

more concrete and sensory phrase, "as long as one of your arms" [33].) The effect is a description both accessible and vivid.

4. We learn that the kid is courteous; he says "please" (5 and 8) and "thanks" (12 and 42). He is, against all odds, a capable, determined fisherman (15, 24, and 47). Both the act of fishing and the fish itself give him tremendous delight. We see his joy in hooking and playing the fish (15 and 22), his pleasure in the narrator's description, and his desire to set the fish free (37).

5. The dialogue in this narrative plays up the shared interests between the narrator and the kid as well as their developing relationship. It gives the essay an informal tone. It brings the reader right into the scene, to see and overhear the event directly. Without the dialogue, the story would have lost its immediacy. The writer would have been reporting or telling us what happened instead of showing us.

6. A view is not just what is seen but a perspective, a way of understanding. The bridge spans the water, but it also represents the connection of respect and understanding that develops between the narrator and the kid.

Classroom Activity Using Organization

Ask students if they see any patterns in the information presented or if they drew any conclusions about these seven states. Depending on their answers (their purposes), students could organize a discussion of these seven states in several ways: (1) chronologically according to the date each state entered the union; (2) spatially from east to west, north to south, and so forth; (3) smallest to largest; (4) by population density; or (5) by effect on national elections. This activity lets students discover that there are always several ways in which they can organize information and that purpose is essential in making an appropriate choice.

Fahrenheit 59: What a Child's Fever Might Tell Us about Climate Change (p. 131)
■ **Audrey Schulman**

Essay Analysis and Discussion

Schulman compares how her son's body and the planet seek to achieve homeostasis through constant self-regulation. Through systems of both positive and negative feedback, both the human body and the earth have various responses to changes in their environments. Schulman argues that we must change our behavior or the planet will stay in a positive feedback mode, heating up until it destroys the most overaggressive microbes, human beings.

Thinking Critically about This Reading

Humans act as overly aggressive microbes in that they are causing the planet to change from a system of negative feedback to one of positive feedback. The planet is no longer just trying to balance itself; it has gone on attack. Most students will be able to relate to the analogy even if they are skeptical about its scientific validity.

Questions for Study and Discussion

1. Schulman begins with a definition of homeostasis, a concept she will build on throughout the essay. Then she uses the analogy of her son's fever to the heating up of the planet. Had she put the example of her son at the end, she would not have been able to build upon the analogy throughout the essay.

2. The analogy of the son's fever has two purposes. First, it builds the structure on which the rest of the essay hangs. Second, it draws in readers who may have been turned off by the more scientific explanation at the beginning. The reference to the son makes the subject easier for nonscientific readers to understand. The relationship between the two subjects is that the human body is like the planet.

3. Homeostasis is the tendency of a system to achieve and maintain internal stability or equilibrium. In human beings, for example, the body is constantly working to achieve an internal temperature of 98.6°F. The blood is rushing to his skin to cool off. She explains this process early because it is a basic and fundamental point in her essay.

4. Negative feedback is when the body makes a change so as to keep itself in balance. When Corey gets overheated from running, his face gets red, which is his body's attempt to cool down and keep him at 98.6°F. The blood is rushing to his skin to cool him off.

5. Normally, when the earth gets warmer, hurricanes increase and the earth attempts to cool itself, just like Corey's blood. When the earth heats up to a certain point, it moves into a positive feedback mode, causing it to break into a fever in an attempt to kill the aggressive microbes. The earth tries to remove what is knocking it out of balance.

6. The son gets a fever because his body wants to rise to a temperature high enough to kill the aggressive microbes in his system. Like Corey's body, the earth is heating up to try to get rid of the species, throwing it out of balance. Students will have various responses to the effectiveness of this analogy.

Classroom Activity Using Organization

The following list includes some suggestions. Students might have acceptable alternatives.

1. What to do when a tornado threatens
   From the most important to the least important
2. What we can do about the homeless
   From the most general to the most specific
3. What we mean by freedom of speech
   From the origins through today
4. A description of a painting
   From the center to the outside
5. How a digital camera works
   Using an analogy of an eyeball
6. Why we need a flat income tax
   Most basic to the most complex reasons
7. What happened at your friend's birthday party
   From the beginning to the end
8. Why we can't let languages become extinct
   From the most objective arguments to the most subjective arguments
9. The case for legalizing drugs
   From the short-term arguments to the long-term arguments

Buying a House (p. 137)
■ Sean Prentiss

Essay Analysis and Discussion

This essay starts in the present, then touches back in time, goes to an imagined or intuited future, and comes back to the present. Students may initially have trouble following this movement. As a class, you could mark where in the essay there are shifts in time. If readers are not paying attention, they could become lost, but the writing has an alternating rhythm that makes sense and works for expressing the themes of the essay, as students might see. The author seems to be using the experience of house hunting to explore the way that we all have many selves and potential selves inside us, many potential destinies. At certain junctures, we must lurch—or think about lurching—toward a new and more mature stage of life, involving risk, commitment, complication, sacrifice, and responsibility. At certain moments, when faced with "a fork in the road," we have to try and balance the possibility of loss, conformity, and diminished horizons with the possibility of love, stability, connection, and happiness. With death looming ahead of us all, at some point, the author seems to pose an important question: How does one find peace and build a good life that admits others, acknowledges parents' and society's expectations, and yet remains true to one's own inherent solitude and restlessness? Within the context of the essay, the house perhaps both triggers these questions and suggests an answer. The

14

rooms of a house are like the rooms of the future—not perfect, not known or fully knowable, but if one makes careful choices and takes a well-intentioned leap, perhaps the future will be a balanced and fulfilling one. Discuss with students the author's strategies for handling the time shifts and for conveying that sense of being "at a fork in the road," which most people can relate to, whether they contemplate home ownership or not.

Thinking Critically about This Reading

A house can simply be a stand-alone dwelling, whereas a home implies a place where one returns to warmth, belongs, and feels welcome. A home has an animated quality, a house an inanimate one. Prentiss's description of the house has more to do with the life that could be lived within its walls and less to do with the structure itself. Prentiss imagines a future within this house, and in that imagining, he creates a home with others.

Questions for Study and Discussion

1. The narration becomes more intimate and revealing as the essay progresses. Prentiss organizes the narration by taking the reader to visit several available houses that he ultimately rejects and then reveals his deepest wishes and thoughts at the last house. His quick review and rejection of the first houses invite the reader to get to know him gradually and lightly, his preferences and journey thus far. By the time he arrives at the house with a porch, readers are prepared for and interested in hearing more about his intimate hopes and thoughts about his future.

2. The italicized sections are usually dialogue, either spoken or inner. They bring the reader into the scene and establish the difference between the reality of what is happening and the thoughts that the author is having about the house. In some instances, italics are used for emphasis (*"Monsters in the Closet. A dream where she couldn't find me."* [paragraph 26]).

3. Other than the kitchen not being in top form, the house has no obvious faults as did the others. The other houses had either crumbling foundations or ruined floors. *626 Lockwood* presented only the realities of Prentiss's own psychology. Is he ready to give up a life of travel and constant moving for dreams that seem to belong more to his parents than himself? He says he only wants a marriage and kids because others his age have them and because his parents would be proud. He seems pressured into the dream of what the house would mean.

4. Prentiss thinks that the porch is where he would be "watching the world go by" (5). In other words, it is where he would watch others live their lives. The porch symbolizes where he would sit peacefully, almost as if in retirement, having the wife and kids because he was supposed to, not because he inherently wanted to have them. The house becomes a symbol of

both the physical reality of his own life and others' expectations. He seems truly drawn to having a house of his own, even if he has not found the place within himself that wants a family.

5. Students' reactions to the ending will vary. Many will be disappointed at not knowing whether or not he bought the house. They are left standing on the front porch with him left to make the decision of whether the expectations of others are worthwhile and the possible benefits of having one's own place. He leaves the reader with his sense of possibility and ambivalence. You might want to ask students how the ending would have felt different if Prentiss had said *will* instead of *can* in the final sentence.

6. Again student answers will vary. He might buy the house just to please his family. Or he might buy it because even though he is not ready for a family, he does seem to want to own his own place. After years of travel, he has committed to a tenure-track job at a university. He might be able to commit to the house, if not yet the uncertainties of love and children.

Classroom Activity Using Organization

Here is one possible organization:

Writing Implements

3 no. 2 pencils
1 mechanical pencil
1 felt-tip pen
1 highlighting marker
3 ballpoint pens

Erasing tools

1 bottle of correction fluid
1 eraser

Office Desk necessities

6 paper clips
7 thumbtacks
1 bottle of glue
2 clasps
25 3- × 5-inch cards
2 rubber bands
1 roll of adhesive tape
2 pairs of scissors

Postal Service Related

1 book mailing bag
3 first-class postage stamps

6 postcard stamps
5 postcards
2 airmail stamps
2 8- × 10-inch manila envelopes
3 business envelopes

Personal Grooming

1 nail file
1 toothbrush
1 nail clipper
1 plastic comb

CHAPTER 6 **Beginnings and Endings**

Of My Friend Hector and My Achilles Heel (p. 154)
■ **Michael T. Kaufman**

Essay Analysis and Discussion

Kaufman's first paragraph is unusual and grabs the reader's attention. Two short sentences admitting prejudice contrast sharply with the finger-pointing, subtle or not, that forms the backbone of most essays about prejudice. Kaufman's story is not dramatic or even noteworthy until the end, but he hooks the reader into bearing with him to find out the nature of his so-called prejudice and stupidity. Have your students write a short personal essay that uses a concise, attention-grabbing first paragraph. Have them discuss the essays and identify the type of essay for which such a first paragraph might be most effective and tell why. Kaufman's ending stays with the reader for two reasons. First, it is a situation with which everyone can empathize because getting back in touch with an old, wrongfully neglected friend is something that most of us should do, but haven't. Second, it is an open-ended conclusion. The reader hopes that perhaps Kaufman will reunite with Hector somehow. Have your students discuss their reaction to the ending. How effective would the essay have been had there been a resolution at the end?

Thinking Critically about This Reading

Kaufman feels the need to apologize for the negative thoughts he had about Hector. Because of Hector's ethnic, financial, and educational background, Kaufman thought he might be a dockworker, for example, not a stage actor. As Kaufman himself states in paragraph 1: "This story is about prejudice and stupidity. My own."

17

Questions for Study and Discussion

1. Such an admission is unusual in a first-person essay, so it grabs the reader's attention and encourages the reader to finish the essay to find out what provoked such a statement. It also leads the reader to pay close attention to Kaufman's writing in the hope of discovering the roots of his stated stupidity. The second part of the question is personal experience.

2. Achilles was a Greek hero who had a weak spot on his heel, a fatal flaw that eventually killed him. Kaufman is referring to his own flaw, which is prejudice.

3. The essay is organized chronologically.

4. Kaufman's purpose is to demonstrate how easy it is to form prejudices and segregate oneself from other people based on assumptions. His organization helps him express his purpose by allowing him to trace when, why, and how his prejudice was formed.

5. Kaufman ignored Hector because he assumed him to be a physical laborer with whom he would have difficulty holding a conversation. It tells him that "tracking," as he calls it, may not be unusual, and it may be damaging to people from the entire range of socioeconomic "tracks."

6. Kaufman's ending is effective because it describes a painful situation with which most people can identify. By keeping the ending open-ended, he emphasizes the ongoing nature of his—and presumably many others'—problem.

Classroom Activity Using Beginnings and Endings

Students readily pick the second paragraph as the one they would use to start an essay. They like its opening sentence, which provokes their curiosity, and the anecdote used to introduce Hugh Troy. The first paragraph has the advantage of using one of Troy's stunts but suffers from an opening sentence that seems to come out of nowhere. The paragraph might make a good ending to an essay about Troy. The third paragraph is simply too dry, too matter-of-fact for a beginning. Although a paragraph like this one is sometimes necessary when writing a brief essay about a famous person, it should not come first.

The Case for Short Words (p. 160)
■ Richard Lederer

Essay Analysis and Discussion

Many writers lose track of what writing is all about somewhere along the way. Instead of a medium of communication, it becomes a medium of vanity, with the writer out to impress readers with craft, not clarity. One of the easiest ways to spot this problem in a piece of writing is in its choice of vocabulary, as *use* becomes *utilize*, *try* becomes *endeavor*, and so on. Lederer's essay addresses this problem in two ways. He presents a standard, although eloquent, plea for the use of short words when long ones are not necessary. He supports his argument with evidence—academic studies that demonstrate that short words provide the foundation for the English language—and examples of great writing and speeches composed entirely of one-syllable words. Much of the effect of his essay, however, comes from how he illustrates his point in a more immediate manner. First, his four paragraphs of single-syllable words do a wonderful job of making his point that you can write well with only short words. Second, by presenting the student essays, he drives home the point that it does not take a great writer to make good use of short words—anyone's writing will benefit from using them when and where appropriate. Ask your students how many saw what Lederer was doing before he told them in the fifth paragraph of his essay. Have them reread the paragraphs. How does Lederer's use of all one-syllable words differ from his standard prose, as seen in the middle of the essay? Which is easier to read and understand?

Thinking Critically about This Reading

Such words can be called the "best" because everyone knows exactly what they are; if you use them, you do not have to worry about how advanced or specialized your audience is. The same advantage holds true for old versus new words. Many students, having studied hard for the SATs and struggled through complex academic essays in school, may believe that having and using a big vocabulary is preferable to using short words. You may want to ask students the difference between having a big vocabulary for reading and using one. You also may want to discuss cases of a larger word that is a good fit and one that is just being used to impress an audience.

Questions for Study and Discussion

1. Lederer's purpose is not to discourage the use of long words, but to encourage the use of more short ones where appropriate, as they can make essays easier to read and understand.
2. By having several quotes from those who are considered among the most effective writers and orators in history, Lederer proves that such great communicators do not seek to use long words just for the sake of showing off. Some of their best work is done with simple tools. The inclusion of the essays by ninth-grade students demonstrates that it does not take the skill and polish of a great writer to use short words with great effectiveness.
3. Students have many choices, such as, "Big words can make the way dark for those who read what you write and hear what you say" (paragraph 2). The metaphor communicates that the use of long words can obscure the

meaning of what a writer wants to say, not to make it easier to understand. "Short words are bright like sparks that glow in the night" (3) contrasts with the former piece of figurative language, communicating that short words are readily understood.

4. Students often feel pressure to come across as learned, formal, or smart in their writing, so they feel pressured to use fancy words. Lederer's point is that great writing often relies on short words, so the success the students have in completing the assignment supports his argument in favor of the use of short words.

5. Lederer's image of the sign will help readers retain the content of his essay. It is something that readers will remember even if they do not care to as they sit down to their next writing assignment.

6. Some answers could be the following:

    a. "Short words are as good as long ones." (1)
        Using a large and advanced vocabulary is not always preferable to using a shorter, more basic vocabulary.

    b. "Use small, old words when you can." (4)
        Use a smaller, more ancient vocabulary when possible.

    c. "They will not let you down." (4)
        Smaller words will rarely disappoint.

    d. "If a long word says just what you want to say, do not fear to use it." (4)
        Never hesitate to select a more advanced word if that word will suffice.

Classroom Activity Using Beginnings and Endings

Also ask students to try reading to one another their second or third paragraph as a possible beginning. Sometimes it takes writers a few paragraphs to warm up. Occasionally, a later paragraph can be the true beginning. You can also ask the students to read their first four paragraphs aloud to one another. The listening students can highlight the sentences that most spoke to them. The writer can then consider using the students' suggestions as a first line and start the introduction from there. This practice is called "line lifting."

Unforgettable Miss Bessie (p. 166)
■ **Carl T. Rowan**

Essay Analysis and Discussion

Rowan's essay offers students the opportunity to analyze the effective use of the dash. Many students have problems recognizing the proper place for this helpful form of punctuation and either use it too much or not at all. Rowan uses it in seven of his paragraphs and for various purposes. Look over these instances with your students and have them identify which of the two most common reasons for using a dash each case falls under.

1. Use dashes to highlight parenthetical material, informal explanations, and afterthoughts that warrant emphasis.
2. Use dashes to signal a dramatic reversal of thought or tone.

When you have finished with Rowan's examples, have students develop sentences of their own, using dashes in each of the ways described.

Thinking Critically about This Reading

Students will say that Miss Bessie taught Rowan about the importance of education, refusal to lower one's standards, and discipline. Miss Bessie provided Rowan with "the push and stimulation of a teacher who truly cared" (paragraph 16). She gave him inspiration and the belief that he could succeed.

Questions for Study and Discussion

1. Miss Bessie gave her students a sense of pride and self-worth by encouraging their talent and curiosity. In opening to them the worlds of literature, writing, self-expression, and a solid notion of this country's time in history, Miss Bessie taught young black children to stretch beyond the limits a segregated world had set for them. Rowan's opening paragraph is an effective beginning because it leads readers to ask, "What else did Miss Bessie teach him?" They need to read on to discover the powerful life lessons this petite dynamo of a teacher gave to Rowan and his peers.
2. The details of Miss Bessie's background appear in paragraphs 9 and 10. Rowan delays presenting this information so that he can first describe what Miss Bessie was like and why he is writing about her. This pattern provides a stimulating opening and establishes a context for the biographical details because it is helpful to know what role Miss Bessie will play in the essay before being given information about her background.
3. In paragraph 1, Rowan describes Miss Bessie as about five feet tall and never more than 110 pounds. In paragraph 4, he notes that she had large brown eyes and, in paragraph 12, that she was "frail-looking." Although these characteristics do not seem to fit the image of the tough and towering figure from Rowan's school days, by the end of the essay they seem less inconsistent with the warm-hearted and compassionate teacher he looks back on as an adult.
4. Students' opinions may vary as to whether Miss Bessie's drinking influences their view of her. Rowan's feeling of a "new sense of equality" suggests that

his discovery that she drank made Miss Bessie more lifelike, dispelling some of the larger-than-life images from his grade-school perception of her, while not diminishing her significance in his life.

5. Rowan's use of dialogue presents a more vivid picture of Miss Bessie's personality. Rather than relying on only a subjective, third-person description of her, Rowan allows the dialogue to provide a few more realistic glimpses into her character.

6. A firm, committed, wise, and caring individual emerges from Rowan's description of Miss Bessie. Some of the words used to convey this impression are *towering, tough* (1); *informed, dedicated, blessing, asset* (8); *essence of pride and privacy* (9); *bearing of dignity* (11); *softness and compassion* (22); *love and motivation, wisdom and influence* (25); and *wise, educated, warm-hearted* (28).

Classroom Activity Using Beginnings and Endings

When students are asked to write alternative beginnings themselves, they find that rhetorical questions, short generalizations, dialogue, and anecdotes seem to work best with Rowan's essay. For example, students offered these two beginnings:

> What for you makes a teacher memorable or remarkable? Miss Bessie was a giant among teachers.

Writing alternative beginnings for their own essays is an activity that frequently sparks significant revision. By looking at their writing from new perspectives, student writers discover for themselves the many possibilities inherent in their subject matter.

An effective way to use this activity is to ask students to locate alternative beginnings within Rowan's essay before writing their own alternative beginnings. Our students nominated several alternatives:

1. Dialogue—paragraphs 2 through 7
2. Anecdote—paragraphs 17 through 19
3. Humor—paragraphs 22 through 24
4. Rhetorical question—paragraph 27
5. Short generalization—paragraph 28

Discuss how each of these alternatives would work as a beginning in the context of Rowan's essay.

Simplicity (p. 176)
■ **William Zinsser**

Essay Analysis and Discussion

Freshmen are often surprised by Zinsser's suggestion to simplify, simplify. Many have come through high school writing courses believing that more is better and that the thesaurus is the basic tool for selecting vocabulary. To reinforce the notion of revising for simplicity's sake, have your students look over Zinsser's sample revision from his manuscript on pages 180–182. Then, using examples from past student papers (or some other suitable source), present students with paragraphs that need simplifying. As students trim words, alter vocabulary, or rearrange sentences, be sure they keep in mind the elements of an effective paragraph: controlling idea, unity, development, and coherence. When they've finished, analyze the deletions and changes and see whether they can identify common types of clutter.

Thinking Critically about This Reading

Zinsser points to "the clotted language of everyday American commerce: the memo, the corporation report, the business letter, the notice from the bank" (paragraph 2). He also gives the example of the airplane pilot, his college's president, and a 1942 blackout order and contrasts them with Thoreau's simplified prose. Zinsser suggests that writers need to think and write clearly, keeping in mind all the things that vie for their audience's short attention span.

Questions for Study and Discussion

1. As Zinsser states in paragraph 1, clutter is a writing disease, the symptoms of which include "unnecessary words, circular constructions, pompous frills, and meaningless jargon." In paragraph 3, Zinsser says that "the secret of good writing is to strip every sentence to its cleanest components." He then proceeds to give examples of "the thousand and one adulterants that weaken the strength of a sentence." Writers need to ask themselves: "What am I trying to say?" and then "Have I said it?" so as to eliminate clutter.

2. Each of Zinsser's paragraphs relates to his topic of clutter in writing and to his purpose of making readers more aware of clutter and its effect on writing. The main idea of each paragraph is as follows:

   1. "Clutter is the disease of American writing."
   2. Most language of American commerce is unnecessarily complicated.
   3. Words that serve no function need to be stripped from prose.

4. People need to express their thoughts in simple, straightforward language.
5. Roosevelt's example of clear English contrasts with the government memo.
6. Simplify as Thoreau does in his writing.
7. Clear thinking leads to clear writing and freedom from clutter.
8. Potential readers have a lot of competition.
9. When readers are lost, it's usually because the writer hasn't been careful enough.
10. Although readers might be forgiving at first, they usually do not stay with writers who make them work too hard.
11. Writers need to know what they are trying to say and cut everything that doesn't contribute to the intended meaning.
12. Thinking clearly is a conscious act that writers must force on themselves.
13. "Writing is hard work."

3. Paragraphs 4 through 6 illustrate the points Zinsser makes in paragraph 3 by providing examples of densely cluttered writing by highly educated people. He then presents simplified versions to underscore what he advocates.

4. Writers must ask themselves constantly: What am I trying to say? Have I said it? Is it clear to someone encountering the subject for the first time? These questions are important to Zinsser because good writing does not come naturally or easily. In addition, the clear thinking that precedes it "is a conscious act that writers must force on themselves."

5. The first paragraph introduces the essay by defining clutter and establishing what Zinsser hopes to eliminate by writing his essay. It provides a necessary context for his thesis about simplicity. The final paragraph is a reminder that good writing does not come naturally but is the result of hard work. It is effective because it reemphasizes the importance of revision to successful writing.

6. "Clear thinking becomes clear writing; one can't exist without the other. It's impossible for a muddy thinker to write good English" (7).

Classroom Activity Using Paragraphs

Students should be immediately impressed by Zinsser's ability to ferret out and eliminate clutter in each of his paragraphs. This skill alone makes the paragraphs clearer and easier to follow because without the clutter Zinsser's craftsmanship shines through. At several points Zinsser edits out whole sentences—sentences that would have weakened the paragraph's unity. For example, in the first new paragraph he cuts the sentence "He *thinks* he knows what the writer is trying to say, but he's not sure," because it does not present an example of carelessness as each of the other sentences in the paragraph does. In that same paragraph, Zinsser uses the word *perhaps* to signal that he is presenting yet another example. Students should note how Zinsser uses the first sentence in each paragraph to refer back to a key idea in the last sentence of the previous paragraph.

One way to conduct this activity in class is to divide the class into groups of two or three and to have each group take responsibility for one of Zinsser's paragraphs. During class discussion, have the groups that worked on the same paragraphs present their findings and conclusions about Zinsser's editing changes.

"I Just Wanna Be Average" (p. 183)
■ Mike Rose

Essay Analysis and Discussion

Students will likely find Rose's tribute to Jack MacFarland entertaining, but some may find it wordy or drawn out. Yet when they study the essay, they will find that each anecdote, each personal reference, and each seemingly casual statement directly relate to the topic Rose wants to present in a particular paragraph. Rose proves that you do not have to be overly concise or conservative in your writing to write an effective essay, but you do need a purpose and need to stick to it in each paragraph. Rose makes MacFarland and his own situation real to the reader while maintaining a flow in his essay that would be impossible to maintain with sloppy paragraphs. Have your students closely examine a paragraph of their choice and explain how each sentence relates to the paragraph's topic. If they write an essay about a teacher, emphasize the importance of using examples and anecdotes to liven up their essay—as long as those examples and anecdotes directly contribute to the paragraph containing them.

Thinking Critically about This Reading

Rose liked getting good grades from MacFarland because, he says, "I suppose I'd been mediocre for too long and enjoyed a public redefinition" (paragraph 5). The grades Rose got from MacFarland meant more to him than other teachers' grades because he respected MacFarland. Unlike other teachers, MacFarland was hip and cool. Ask students to point to specific passages where Rose writes about MacFarland's cool style.

Questions for Study and Discussion

1. The title gives the reader a sense of just how much Rose's standards were raised by MacFarland. By the end of the essay, Rose obviously rises well above the average in a number of areas—he has exceeded his academic dreams.

2. MacFarland is a slob with wrinkled pants, a sorry tie, and stained teeth. Obviously, his abilities as a teacher have nothing to do with the way he looks.

3. (1) Jack MacFarland looked awful, but he was a very good teacher. (2) MacFarland's lectures were well crafted and intellectually stimulating, and his course covered a lot of ground. (3) He was able to handle the difficult students and earn everyone's respect. (4) MacFarland inspired Rose to work hard and do well. (5) Good grades from MacFarland were things of value. (6) MacFarland encouraged Rose to work to get into college. (7) MacFarland succeeded in helping Rose go to college.

4. Rose's second paragraph can be divided into two parts. In the first four sentences, he discusses how MacFarland built up his students' knowledge of Western intellectual history. This background or overview material is necessary preparation for the analytical work that is discussed in the next four sentences of the paragraph. Rose's use of the pronouns "he" (MacFarland) and "we" (students) shows how the teacher led the way in the activities described in both parts of the paragraph. Rose's detailed accounting of authors, works, concepts, and activities prepares readers for the last sentence of that paragraph, "The man immersed us in language."

5. The transition between paragraphs 2 and 3 has to do with language — Rose's somewhat idyllic view in paragraph 2 and the real world of Mercy High in paragraph 3. The transition between paragraphs 3 and 4 brings the reader to what MacFarland did for Rose in particular. Rose shows what MacFarland did in class and how he interacted with others before he begins an in-depth account of his own relationship with MacFarland.

6. Rose introduces the reader to real people, kids like those everyone knows in high school. It makes the essay more entertaining, and it gives the reader a way to see what MacFarland had to contend with. By making them real to the reader, Rose shows the interaction MacFarland had with a variety of students and the respect he earned from all.

7. Rose has difficulty getting into college because his grades are awful. He makes it by doing well in MacFarland's class and having him pull strings at his alma mater.

Classroom Activity Using Paragraphs

Once students select their topic sentences, have them make a list of all the details that come to mind that could be used in a paragraph. For example, for the topic sentence, "Signs of the sanitation strike were evident everywhere," a student's list might include "a discarded mattress, overflowing trash cans, littered streets, the smells of decaying garbage in dumpsters, piles of plastic trash bags curbside, rats venturing out in daylight, and flies everywhere." Next, have students write their paragraphs using only those details needed to show, demonstrate, or support the idea in the topic sentence. Finally, have several students read their paragraphs aloud—or better yet, put them on transparencies—for the class to discuss for unity, coherence, and development.

The Last Shot (p. 189)
■ Tobias Wolff

Essay Analysis and Discussion

In this essay, Wolff wants to communicate a memory and provide an image of someone he remembers. Of course, writing can capture only so much; memories are unreliable and inexact, and writers must selectively add details. Ask students how successfully Wolff creates an image of Hugh. Which details created that image? Wolff did not indulge in a lengthy physical description of Hugh. Why not? Why do students think Wolff selected the details he did? When writing about someone who has died, the writer has the burden or responsibility of representing someone who can no longer represent himself or herself.

Thinking Critically about This Reading

Student opinions will vary. Those who argue for allowing the military to advertise might include arguments such as no one today could be oblivious to the realities of war, as they were in Orwell's generation, with today's in-depth news coverage and so many men coming home maimed. They might also argue that the advertising is not untrue, saying that enlistees will often have the opportunity to see the world, get and education, and so forth. Those arguing against advertising might say the promotions are too seductive and an uneducated person might be seduced. They could argue that, like cigarette ads, military ads ought to be banned from radio, TV, and cinema advertising. They may argue that any product and service that dramatically increases risk of death or ill health ought not to be promoted.

Questions for Study and Discussion

1. Wolff's thesis argues against the promotion of dying young as something to be idealized. In his words, "Figure of speech or not, he meant it, and anyway the words could not be separated from their martial beat and the rhetoric that promotes dying young as some kind of good deal" (paragraph 2).
2. Wolff is angry at Orwell's promotion of dying young as superior to dying of old age.
3. Here are two example paragraphs.

   Paragraph 4
   - Yes. The paragraph has a clear topic sentence: "Instead of remembering Hugh as I knew him, I too often think of him in terms of what he never had a chance to be."

- Yes. Wolff then provides clear examples of the fantasy life Hugh missed by dying young.
- Yes. The paragraph is unified, discussing only the evolution of a life that Hugh missed, a life that teaches us who we are.
- Yes. The paragraph is coherent. Wolff's use of simple, clear sentences and short paragraphs to make his point makes this section coherent.

Paragraph 6
- Yes. "Hugh loves to jump."
- Yes. He develops the paragraph clearly, slowly teasing out to the reader the scene of the two men parachuting out of the plane—one into his life, and the other to his death. Some readers might struggle initially to understand that the scene takes place on a plane in Vietnam.
- Yes. The paragraph is unified. It starts with Hugh's love of jumping and ends with him actually jumping.
- Yes. The paragraph is coherent. All the sentences relate to the topic sentence and larger theme of the essay.

4. The first sentences of each of Wolff's paragraphs tend to be a direct response to the last sentence in each preceding paragraph. For example, he starts paragraph 2 with "It stopped me cold." This technique allows Wolff to transition from Orwell's article to his own feelings about the larger issue of promoting a youthful death. Paragraph 3 begins, "Several men I knew were killed in Vietnam." This statement transitions the essay from his personal response to Orwell's comment, asserts him as an authority, and transitions to the discussion of Vietnam. The least smooth transition is between paragraphs 4 and 5. He moves from discussing life as a way to finding out who we are into his mistake of thinking about Hugh as an absence. Perhaps he could have smoothed out this transition. He seems to be saying that because Hugh was deprived of a full life, he could never know himself and therefore neither could Wolff. He seems to be saying that instead of focusing on the lack of what Hugh became, he would focus on what he was during his time on the planet.

5. He switches into the present tense to bring the reader into the last moments of Hugh's life and the last moments they shared. The present tense escalates the excitement and the tension of the final jump. Wolff is no longer retelling the story; he relives it and brings the reader with him. This technique also helps the reader reevaluate Orwell's comment about the benefits of dying young. The present tense allows the reader to feel the intensity of having to jump out of that plane. Hugh's final question, "Are we having fun?" forces the reader to ask himself or herself if that experience sounded fun or as glorious as Orwell suggested.

6. Students may have different interpretations. The last shot could mean the shot that ended a youthful life. The last shot also reminds readers that

28

Hugh did not get any other "shots" at life. He had just his short experience. It begs the question, why did Orwell see this way to die as such a wonderful one?

Classroom Activity Using Paragraphs

One possible order is the following:

1. Athletes who overtrain find it difficult to get into the flow.
2. PGA golfer Fred Divot learned the hard way what overtraining could do.
3. "I was playing well, so I thought with a bit more practice, I could start winning on tour," Divot recalled.
4. "Two weeks later, all I could think about was the mechanics, and I couldn't hit a fairway to save my life."
5. Athletes think about mechanics (left hemisphere) rather than feel (right hemisphere), and they lose the ability to achieve peak performance.
6. Divot's case is typical, and most researchers believe that too much repetition makes it difficult for the athlete to reduce left-hemisphere brain activity.

CHAPTER 8 **Transitions**

On Being 17, Bright, and Unable to Read (p. 197)
■ David Raymond

Essay Analysis and Discussion

Raymond writes openly and honestly about his experience growing up and struggling with dyslexia. Although he was relieved to learn that he had a learning disability and was not "dumb," he feared that his classmates would ridicule him if they learned that he was "going to a school for the retarded" (paragraph 10) to attend special education classes. Raymond's use of transitions is fairly sophisticated, so you might want to walk students through the essay once and, pointing out the transitions between paragraphs, answer Study and Discussion question 1 as a class. This exercise will help students understand that they may incorporate transitions in their own writing that are not dictated by a predetermined list of words and phrases.

Thinking Critically about This Reading

When asked, Raymond says he goes "to Mars" (12) when he leaves class to receive special instruction. He did not want his classmates to know that he was taking special education classes at another school. He states: "The bus also picked up emotionally disturbed kids and retarded kids. It was like going to a school for the retarded" (10). He was afraid that he would be considered retarded, a label he believed was worse than the label "dyslexic."

Questions for Study and Discussion

1. Raymond uses the following transitional devices:
   - Concession between paragraphs 1 and 2
   - Repeated key ideas between paragraphs 2 and 3
   - Concession between paragraphs 3 and 4
   - Reference to time between paragraphs 4 and 5
   - Repeated key ideas between paragraphs 5 and 6
   - Pronoun reference between paragraphs 6 and 7
   - Repeated key ideas between paragraphs 7 and 8
   - Reference to time between paragraphs 8 and 9
   - Repeated key ideas between paragraphs 10 and 11, 11 and 12, 12 and 13, 13 and 14, 14 and 15, and 15 and 16

2. Other examples include "but from where I sit," "unless you've been there," "I wish I were dead," "I guess I couldn't read," and "I didn't talk as good as other kids." These colloquialisms are the authentic expressions of a 17-year-old youth, and they add to the realism and credibility of the essay.

3. Raymond's tone is intimate, sincere, and although informal, serious enough to establish his central point. The colloquial expression suggests that his reflections are honest.

4. Dyslexia is a learning disorder in which the brain cannot interpret spatial relationships or has trouble distinguishing between aural and visual information. The definition is not included because the essay is not about dyslexia. Raymond is writing about the effect on a child of being labeled different or stupid.

5. Raymond's purpose for telling his story is to explain to teachers and parents what it is like to be dyslexic so that they will treat other children with this difficulty compassionately.

6. Raymond's story warns us that negative early-childhood experiences can have a devastating effect on a child's self-esteem, academic performance, and achievement, and that this effect can define us as adults.

Classroom Activity Using Transitions

The correct order for the sentences is 6, 4, 8, 3, 9, 2, 11, 1, 12, 5, 10, 7. Engage students in a discussion of the language cues that helped them arrange the sentences in a logical order. Students will readily point to transitions like *first* and *however*, the pronoun *this*, the repetition of key ideas such as "wetting down the surface" and "foreign material," and the organizational device "three steps."

Becoming a Writer (p. 203)
■ Russell Baker

Essay Analysis and Discussion

Few have gone through school without knowing a teacher like Baker's Mr. Fleagle—earnest, interested in his subject, eager to teach, but unable to communicate the joy of the subject to the class. The effectiveness of Baker's essay rests on his ability to describe Mr. Fleagle, and his description in paragraphs 2 and 3 is amusing, devastating, and full of imagery. Students should have a clear notion of Mr. Fleagle's appearance, personality, and mannerisms from the description, and it should communicate to them the lesson Baker himself learns in the course of the essay—good writing can be funny and informal if it is clear and written with a purpose. It is through having so thoroughly established Mr. Fleagle as inept that Baker can make the ending surprising and effective, and it is easy for the reader to share Baker's joy and surprise. The paragraph transitions become particularly important in the telling of the development of the essay and its subsequent fate. Baker ushers the reader along in chronological order, but by no means is it a plodding account. Baker bases his transitions on emotions and feelings, going from the joy of writing the essay, to the anxiety of waiting for it to come back, to the joy of having it read. The reader can easily follow the progression, and the emotion-based transitions carry the reader on the same roller coaster Baker endured to the end.

Thinking Critically about This Reading

Seeing his classmates' reaction to his essay encouraged him: "I was feeling pure ecstasy at this startling demonstration that my words had the power to make people laugh" (paragraph 12). He felt that he had "discovered a calling" (12). Baker thought so highly of Fleagle because he had "opened a door for me" (13).

Questions for Study and Discussion

1. Baker's transitional expressions, repeated key words and ideas, and pronoun references have been underlined in the following transcription of paragraphs 1 and 2.

    The notion of becoming a writer had flickered off and on in my head . . . but it wasn't until my third year in high school that the possibility took hold. Until then I'd been bored by everything associated with English courses. I found English grammar dull and baffling. I hated the assignments to turn out "compositions," and went at them like heavy labor, turning out laden, lackluster paragraphs that were agonies for teachers to read and for me to write. The classics thrust on me to read seemed as deadening as chloroform.

31

When our class was assigned to Mr. Fleagle for third-year English I anticipated another grim year in that dreariest of subjects. <u>Mr. Fleagle</u> was notorious among City students for dullness and inability to inspire. He was said to be <u>stuffy, dull, and hopelessly out of date</u>. To me he looked to be sixty or seventy and prim to a fault. He wore <u>primly</u> severe eyeglasses, his wavy hair was <u>primly</u> cut and <u>primly</u> combed. He wore *prim* vested suits with neckties blocked <u>primly</u> against the collar buttons of his <u>primly</u> starched white shirts. He had a <u>primly</u> pointed jaw, a <u>primly</u> straight nose, and a <u>prim</u> manner of speaking that was so correct, so gentlemanly, that he seemed a comic antique.

2. Make sure students note how Baker links the paragraphs to each other so that they flow chronologically without resorting to a plodding "Then I did this, then he did that" progression many students fall into. Baker uses some basic transitions—"This title," "When I finished it," "And he started to read," for example—but they are skillfully woven into the emotion of the story, so they lead the reader on without interfering with the flow of the narrative.

3. Baker's description of Mr. Fleagle paints an extremely clear picture of a teacher who will have trouble communicating with adolescents. Stuffy, prim, correct, antique—all are damning adjectives for teenagers. The repeated use of the word *prim* emphasizes the character of someone who appears out of touch with students; he sounds like the male equivalent of a stuffy old aunt whom children never want to visit because they must dress in uncomfortable clothes and sit up straight for what seems like hours on end. The description is important for the essay because it maximizes the effect of the later revelation Baker has in Fleagle's class. The man described in paragraph 2 seems incapable of inspiring anyone to do anything.

4. Baker writes about the art of eating spaghetti based on a happy memory of an evening spent eating spaghetti with relatives. He writes about it because he wants to and because it brings back good feelings for him. He does not want to turn his essay in because he thinks it violates all rules of formal composition—it is not respectable enough for Mr. Fleagle.

5. Mr. Fleagle had demonstrated to Baker the power that his writing could have: It could make people laugh and enjoy the experience of reading or hearing it. Baker's prejudice that writing is not honest work made it difficult for him to think of writing as a career.

Classroom Activity Using Transitions

The lack of transitions between the three paragraphs in the exercise is painfully obvious, but writing them for text that is already there will teach students the kind of information and the techniques for linking paragraphs that are necessary for smooth transitions. There are no absolute right or wrong answers, but when a student reads the completed passage aloud, it should flow from paragraph to paragraph and be easy to follow. You might want to allow a little more time for this activity than usual, as it may take students a while to create effective transitions.

The Magic of the Family Meal (p. 208)
■ Nancy Gibbs

Essay Analysis and Discussion

Nancy Gibbs discusses a topic familiar to many students: the changing nature of the American family, especially in relation to how we eat. She compares the modern-day family meal with that of the *Leave It to Beaver* family, an idealized television family from the 1950s. Instead of eating together, today many families eat separately or on the run. Much of the essay revolves around a study conducted by Columbia University that draws on a decade of data. The study by the Center on Addiction and Substance Abuse demonstrates the many benefits of eating together: Children abuse fewer substances, they perform better in school, they wait longer before having sex, and families tend to eat better. Gibbs points out that children benefit from family meals even if the conversation is not perfect or each person seems to be mentally somewhere else. Children, even teenagers, seem to benefit from this time together.

Thinking Critically about This Reading

Given the statistics about broken homes, many students may initially be surprised that most Hispanic families eat together. On second reflection, students may also remember that in some cultures—including French, Italian, and Spanish—eating with the family still plays an important role. It was Americans who invented the frozen dinner and quick meals. Students also may be surprised to learn that children who have dinner with their parents do 40 percent better in school than those who do not. Students may think differently not only about ethnicity and family meals, but also about how they want to raise their own children. They may also challenge some of Gibbs's statistics and conclusions, question whether the issue of academic success and correlations with ethnicity might be more complicated than presented here, and be inspired to do more research on line.

Questions for Study and Discussion

1. At the idealized family dinner, the mother is wearing an apron and pearls, the father a sweater and tie, "The napkins are linen, the children are scrubbed, steam rises from the greenbean casserole, and even the dog listens intently to what is being said" (paragraph 1). At the family dinner table, wisdom is passed down, expectations are set, confessions are made,

forgiveness is given, and relationships are repaired. When Gibbs compares this idealized version to worship, she means that this ideal picture has as many rules as a religious ceremony. How one is to behave, the order of events, the placement of objects, and the way roles are clearly set are all defined; for example, the woman cooks, the man carves, the boy clears, the girl washes. Like a religious ceremony, this idealized dinner has a deep spiritual component. Idealized tribal meetings promote profound inner adjustments by increasing wisdom, setting expectations, and promoting forgiveness. These qualities are also often the goals of many religious ceremonies.

2. Teenagers who eat with their families more often are less likely "to smoke, drink, do drugs, get depressed, develop eating disorders and consider suicide, and . . . more likely . . . to do well in school, delay having sex, eat their vegetables, learn big words, and know which fork to use" (4). This practice of eating together protects teenagers from many of the dangerous effects of peer pressure and outer society, giving them the foundations they need to become stable, healthy adults.

3. Student opinions will vary regarding the importance to older kids of eating with their parents. Teenagers are often busy with school activities, sports, and social events. Although they often attempt to minimize parental contact, this avoidance may be because they need it most. Some students may suggest that the family is not a "protected" environment if the parents speak negatively to their children. In some cases, perhaps, teenagers need some adult support while wanting to limit their exposure to their family. Perhaps eating with a friend's family could also have benefits, as could eating with any adult or group who cares about them. Some students may also say that teenagers need to prepare to eat without their families, since they will soon be in college. They may claim that teenagers need time to solidify their own identities.

4. Students may be surprised by the finding in paragraph 6, that "families with the least educated parents, for example, eat together the most; parents with less than a high school education share more meals with their kids than do parents with high school diplomas or college degrees" (6). The *Leave It to Beaver* family seemed educated and white, and these studies show that perhaps more immigrant and less-educated families are benefiting from these dinners. Students might be surprised at how effective family dinners are. They may also wonder why, if all these less-educated families have dinner together, that demographic still seems to have higher-than-average rates of drug abuse and teenage pregnancy. Students might also react positively to the finding that it does not seem to matter whether the family dinner is perfect as long as it occurs. This finding takes the pressure off and allows families to just be together without all the predefined roles.

5. Gibbs uses a repeated idea from paragraph 1 when starting paragraph 2. She refers to "that ideal," the ideal explained in the introduction. In the

beginning of paragraph 8, she refers to the "tidy picture" she created in paragraph 7. Paragraph 7 ends with a perfect picture of a family dinner, and paragraph 8 begins with a reference to all of the factors that have worked to destroy that picture. Between paragraphs 8 and 9, she uses the transitional expression "But something. . . ." Between paragraphs 10 and 11, she uses a repeated idea. In paragraph 10, she cites the increase in frequency of adolescents eating with their families and starts paragraph 11 referring directly to "that rise." She begins paragraph 12 by summarizing and naming a concept introduced in paragraph 11, and she repeats and develops it. The "food-court mentality" is her name for the final idea presented in paragraph 11. To move from paragraph 12 to paragraph 13, Gibbs uses the transitional word "beyond." Each strategy summarizes the ideas presented in the previous paragraph while moving the reader forward, introducing a new concept or developing the one that precedes it. These transitions also help her go from her specific examples at the end of each paragraph and place them within a larger context or discussion in the next. She accomplishes these transitions by making a more general claim or summary at the start of the new paragraph, getting increasingly specific, and then starting the next one with a broader discussion of the topic. The pattern then repeats.

6. Gibbs claims that the following factors led to the demise of the family dinner: working parents, "kids shuttling between sports practices or attached to their screens at home, finding a time for everyone to sit around the same table, eating the same food and listening to one another" (8). She also cites the invention of the microwave as encouraging people to consider cooking a waste of time.

7. Student opinions will vary. This concept might be new to students who did not grow up this way—even sitcoms show families eating together less and less, so students have been exposed to fewer idealized versions as well. At heart, it is something many people crave, even if it is not something they have experienced. Whether or not one likes pot roast, a meal shared is often far more rewarding than eating alone, when we often eat quickly and barely taste the food. Buddha made a comment that said, in essence, that if people knew the power of sharing, they would never let a meal go by without sharing it in some way. Many students will probably remember the stress and joys of holiday meals and use these memories as reference points.

Classroom Activity Using Transitions

The correct order for the sentences in E. B. White's paragraph is 4, 2, 5, 1, 3. The sentences in the paragraph follow in chronological order from that first summer in 1904 to the present. Students will point to the time markers "1904," "returned," "since," and "a few weeks ago." White uses pronouns skillfully as well; he moves from the family experience ("we" and "us") to the personal experience

("I"). Finally, White uses subtle references to previous ideas to link sentences together. For example, when he states "We returned there summer after summer," we know that the place he is referring to is "a lake in Maine," and we know that "this feeling" in sentence 3 relates back to his "wish for the placidity of a lake in the woods."

CHAPTER 9 **Effective Sentences**

Childhood (p. 222)
■ Alice Walker

Essay Analysis and Discussion

Alice Walker writes about some of her happiest memories of childhood through a description of her experiences gardening as an adult. We learn that Walker loves growing her own vegetables, and she shares with the reader what she loves about the process. She then drifts back to the past, explaining that her farming passion comes from her childhood as part of a farming family. But Walker's daughter is already thirty-one, and Walker hasn't yet passed this knowledge on to her, although she is eager to do so. Walker uses sentences of varying length and pattern. As a result, her essay is interesting rather than monotonous.

Thinking Critically about This Reading

Walker suggests that our happy childhood memories help frame what we love and appreciate as adults. You may want to ask students to consider if much of the wonder Walker experienced was the wonder of childhood. That is, was everything so astonishing simply because it was new to her? Or does Walker effectively communicate that farming has a kind of magic in and of itself and that the reason she finds it satisfying as an adult is that growing food is a truly miraculous process? You could also ask students if they think most processes could be seen as miraculous when seen through the eyes of a contented child.

Questions for Study and Discussion

1. Walker's thesis is in the last sentence of paragraph 3: "The experience I had had digging the potatoes, before turning them into half of a delicious meal, was one I wanted my daughter to know."
2. Walker uses sentence variety in her first four paragraphs, alternating between descriptive and narrative sentences of varying length. She uses *subordination, passive voice, periodic sentences,* and *dramatically short sentences.* Her dramatically short sentences include:

a. "She wasn't sure" (1). This emphasizes the gap in experience between Walker and her daughter and encourages the reader to consider how potatoes look.

b. "It had been years since I planted potatoes" (2). This provides a nice pause after her description of the potato crop and tells the reader that planting potatoes was a kind of return to herself and her past.

c. "Then I remembered my potatoes!" (3). This exclamation propels the story forward. It moves the reader from her description of the vegetables she wishes to bring to the city into the action required to harvest the potatoes.

d. "We owned a beautiful handcrafted butter press" (4). This short, sweet sentence demonstrates her appreciation not just for the vegetables, but for all of the well-made objects that play a part in the farming process.

3. The long sentence at the beginning of paragraph 5 emphasizes the amount of produce Walker will bring with her to the city. It also helps reinforce how much farming she has done and what abundance her garden produces. Because the sentence is mostly a list of familiar items, most readers will find it easy to follow.

4. Walker uses longer sentences that follow one another smoothly, reemphasizing time and the gentle handing down of something so taxing as farming. It demonstrates that something large, when done consistently, becomes casual and manageable, enabling it to be repeated year after year. She repeats the word year to give readers a sense of time. She uses such words as *magic, extraordinary, wonderment,* and *heroic* to reemphasize the special nature of farming and her family's relationship to it.

5. Walker found harvesting potatoes to be one of the great joys of her life and one that connected her with her familial roots. Potatoes are root vegetables and provide a symbol for teaching her daughter about her own roots.

6. This activity was one that they both loved and shared. They both had the same sense of wonder and astonishment. Walker successfully passed on some of her family history to her adult daughter, showing that it is never too late to find your roots. They found their common ground, and Walker was able to give her daughter something she could most meaningfully share only with her own children.

7. Some students may claim that her question to her daughter in paragraph 1 demonstrated her own knowledge of farming. Few people have seen potatoes in the earth.

Classroom Activity Using Effective Sentences

Although this paragraph describes a dramatic event, it is written in a way that makes it boring and difficult to read. The sentence structure is monotonously consistent, and although all the necessary information is included, it is presented in such a way that the mundane has equal footing with the dramatic and unusual. You might wish to read the paragraph aloud to the class as it stands and then read the students' revised paragraphs aloud when they are done. Hearing the passage in both forms will give students an auditory reference for what they need to do to create interesting and effective sentences.

Salvation (p. 228)
■ Langston Hughes

Essay Analysis and Discussion

In addition to Hughes's use of different sentence lengths and patterns in this essay, he varies the manner of his material, particularly for the scene at the church. To add a sense of the revival meeting's liveliness, he includes bits of conversation that enhance the essay's main idea. In paragraph 3, he presents the preacher's words; in paragraph 6, Westley's whispered mutterings; and in paragraphs 8 through 10, an exchange between the minister and Hughes's aunt. To illustrate the effects of these passages, read the essay aloud to your students and ask them to pay attention to what the dialogue contributes. Your discussion should especially focus on the dialogue's relation to the first and last paragraphs, and on how the inclusion of conversation helps convey Hughes's central idea. Students should also notice that he includes only enough dialogue to serve his purpose.

Thinking Critically about This Reading

Hughes cries because he had lied to the congregation about seeing Jesus, because he regrets not seeing Jesus, and because he now doubts that Jesus exists at all. The irony is that Hughes's "salvation from sin" was based on a lie.

Questions for Study and Discussion

1. According to Hughes, salvation is being "saved from sin" when Jesus and the Holy Ghost come into your life. Young Langston "wanted to see Jesus." However, his salvation was more important to his aunt, who cared about his soul and didn't want to be embarrassed in front of the congregation by his being the only one left who had not been saved. Hughes expects to be saved because his aunt and the other townspeople had built up the expectation during the weeks of preparation for the revival meeting. In paragraph 3 we see the various appeals made by the preacher, and in paragraph 4 we see how the preacher's appeals are reinforced by the prayers and songs of the congregation.

2. Have students read portions of Hughes's essay aloud so that they can hear the rhythms that his sentences create. They'll see how the short, dramatic sentences punctuate the events of the evening, engaging readers in the emotions of the moment. Longer sentences, such as the one that begins paragraph 3, reinforce the ebb and flow of the preaching and singing at the revival meeting. Others, such as the third sentence in paragraph 11, reflect the unfolding of Hughes's thinking as he tries to decide whether to stand up at the revival meeting or what the whole experience means in the end.

3. If these two sentences had been combined, the dramatic effect of the reversal of thought and statement would have been lost.

4. The coordinating conjunctions in paragraph 3 are *and*, *and*, *and*, *and*, and *but*. Hughes uses coordinating conjunctions throughout his essay. When he wants to link closely related actions and not give any one of them emphasis, he does so in a long sentence. When he wants to link closely related ideas but give emphasis to each idea, he uses short sentences that begin with coordinating conjunctions.

5. The subordinating conjunctions in paragraph 15 are *for*, *for*, *because*, *because*, *because*, *that*, *that*, *that*, *that*, and *since*. In this last paragraph Hughes reflects on the experience and, therefore, makes explicit connections.

6. Some of the words Hughes uses to remind us that we are at a revival meeting are *sin*, *mourners' bench*, *preached*, *sermon*, *hell*, *prayed*, *Jesus*, *congregation*, and *wail*. In addition, Hughes uses traditional religious figures of speech such as "to bring the young lambs to the fold," "when you were saved you saw a light," "lower lights are burning," and "all the new young lambs were blessed in the name of God."

Classroom Activity Using Effective Sentences

The six sets of short sentences can be rewritten as follows:

1. I can take the 6:30 express train or catch the 7:00 bus.
2. Miriam was tired after working all weekend on her research paper, for which she interviewed five people.
3. Juan did not have time to work out at the gym for over a month because his new job kept him busy every day.
4. Completely restored for the nation's 200th birthday, the Statue of Liberty, a gift of the French government over 120 years ago, welcomes newcomers to America.
5. The starting center on the basketball team, Carla is a tall, strong team player.
6. Betsy loves Bach's music, and she also likes Scott Joplin.

Have students put their rewrites on the board and discuss the ways in which each of the sets of sentences can be combined.

Volar (p. 233)
■ Judith Ortiz Cofer

Essay Analysis and Discussion

Preteens are beginning to enter the more adult world, but often like to keep a toehold in childhood world of fantasy. It's a lot to give up. The daughter's fantasy world experienced through comic books enables her to keep that foothold in fantasy. The essay shows that it is not just children who need dreams and fantasy to handle the reality of daily life. The mother too has her dreams of returning home and wishes she could fly. You may want to ask students what dreams they keep to get them through some of the tedium or challenges of daily life.

Thinking Critically about This Reading

When moving from one country to another, people often experience culture shock in the following areas: food, language, weather, etiquette (social graces), educational system, value of family, daily stress levels, speed of daily life. In addition, the role of honor, the role of money, and other values could all be different.

Questions for Study and Discussion

1. *Volar* means "to fly" in Spanish. It refers to both the mother and the daughter's shared fantasy that they could fly beyond their current circumstances. The daughter is seeking more power in her own American life, and her mother is seeking a way back to Puerto Rico, her home country.

2. For the daughter, flying provides freedom and the ability to affect others over whom she has no control, such as her landlord. For the mother, flying signifies her desire to return to her home country.

3. Most of Cofer's sentences are of similar length. She uses four short sentences:

   a. "Sleek and hard as a supersonic missile."
      This short sentence itself is an example of something sleek, hard, and supersonic. It shows how a superhero has to be, compact and striking.

   b "I played a trick on him."
      The short sentence here reminds the reader that the writer is a child, a seemingly innocent one.

   c. "Not abruptly."
      The phrase highlights that her mother is not angry with her husband for not being able to pay for the plane tickets.

   d. "A birthday gift."
      This phrase tells the reader that others think that the mother needs to pray for grace and patience. Presumably whoever gave her the gift wanted her to focus on it instead of on the frustrations of living so far from Puerto Rico. It was not her asking.

40

4. The long sentence at the end of paragraph 1 highlights Cofer's transition from her superhero dream space where everything was to her choosing, back to her daily life, one in which everything from her furniture to her appearance were not under her control. Student opinion may vary regarding the sentence's difficulty. Cofer's writing is fairly simple. The sentence provides a good example for simple longer sentences, especially for students prone to short sentences.

5. The dashes and semicolons give the writing the energy of the child narrator. Children often talk quickly and in run-on sentences. Their enthusiasm tends to keep the sentence going. Semicolons and dashes give the narrative a giddy, playful quality.

6. Cofer uses sentence fragments to indicate importance and to slow the reader down. A fragment is a signal to the reader that she is saying something vital to the story or vital to her mother's character. In the last paragraph, she uses two fragments: "Not abruptly," to show how her mother moved through the kitchen and the slow, calculated movements of the moment; and "A birthday gift," signaling the importance placed on the origins of the clock that her mother was given, representing patience and grace.

Classroom Activity Using Effective Sentences

Bonnie wore red shorts with pockets.

1. To be in the woods before the sun came up, the deer hunter woke up at 5 a.m. and ate a quick breakfast of coffee, juice, and cereal.
2. My grandparents, who played golf every weekend for years, stopped playing last year and now really miss it.
3. When you fly over any major city and look out the airplane's window, you will be appalled by the number of tall smokestacks you will see.
4. Because it did not rain for more than three months, most of the crops in the region failed, bringing some farmers to the brink of bankruptcy.
5. Every day of the week I go to work, exercise, shower, exercise, relax, and eat a light, low-fat dinner.

CHAPTER 10 **Writing with Sources**

Praise the Humble Dung Beetle (p. 255)
■ **Sharon Begley**

Essay Analysis and Discussion

Begley integrates numerous sources without overwhelming or distracting readers from her main point. She also integrates quotations and paraphrasing without losing her own voice. How does she do it? All the quotes used support her main defense of the importance of the less-loved endangered species. She launches into a discussion not about the centers for biodiversity, but rather about the importance of conservation. She refers to biologists whose thoughts and opinions can help bridge the gap between animal and human worlds, such as through the analogy between ecosystems and airplanes. By selecting sources carefully and seamlessly integrating them into her essay, Begley offers a persuasive and authoritative essay in just seven paragraphs.

Thinking Critically about This Reading

Begley wants to convince us of all three purposes; by informing us about beetles and other invertebrates, she is better able to argue for the inclusion of more plants and invertebrates on the list of endangered species. She thinks that we might be convinced to include them if we became better informed. Most people know little about the ecosystems around them; therefore, she hopes to change people's beliefs through education. Because readers come with all different levels of knowledge and experience, Begley must educate her readers enough to convince them and must also provide examples that are not too redundant or basic for more sophisticated readers.

Questions for Study and Discussion

1. Begley claims, with the help of biologist Sacha Spector, that the dung beetle plays a vital role in the larger ecosystem. Dung beetles wrap up and bury animal feces, and, in so doing, they reintroduce nutrients into the soil, prevent disease-carrying pests from living in them, and bury seeds that grow into a variety of plants and trees. To Spector, the dung beetle is not just a passing interest or fodder for an interesting magazine article, but a life's passion. Begley lets readers know that this topic is important enough for there to be a department of invertebrates at the Center for Biodiversity and Conservation. Spector not only believes that these invertebrates are important, he gets excited about them. Begley hopes that Spector's enthusiasm will rub off on readers and lead them to find compassion for endangered animals beyond the elephant and polar bear.

2. Begley thinks that it is a shame people prefer the megafauna to the smaller creatures, which are also wonderfully interesting and useful. She finds this bias dangerous because without these creatures, the ecosystem would be disjointed—plants wouldn't be pollinated, seeds wouldn't get buried, and so on. Also, these creatures have evolved sophisticated mechanisms for survival that can inform and inspire humans, helping us be more energy efficient and create new and better products. Begley quotes Kiernan Suckling to substantiate her claim, stating that these plants and invertebrates "feed the entire planet, stabilize the soil, and make all life possible" (paragraph 2). Had Begley made this claim, the reader might find her passionate but

not authoritative. Begley gets her authority by quoting this cofounder of the Center for Biological Diversity.

3. Begley paraphrases the point of each authority and then gives a direct quote. This practice prepares readers for the ideas the quotes will introduce. Because it is Begley who has the relationship with the reader, these introductions encourage the reader to listen to the authorities. In addition to giving each person's name, she also cites the professional position held by each scientist, thus simultaneously introducing the reader to the idea of biodiversity organizations. These paraphrases further substantiate her point that we need to protect the entire ecosystem. If there are organizations dedicated solely to biodiversity and others sponsored by such renowned organizations as the Museum of Natural History, surely this issue must be a significant one.

4. She mentions the Nambian beetle, which pulls water from the fog and inspired designs now used in cooling towers, industrial condensers, and dry farming regions. The spiral in the shell of the mollusk, which efficiently moves water, inspired new fans and components in computers and air conditioners. Mussels have a protein that scientists are trying to replicate to create a new superglue. The burying beetle can smell death from two miles away within an hour of the death. Quoting Quentin Wheeler's point that the burying beetle's sense of smell could be used to find earthquake victims makes all this information important and real. Sure, it would be nice to have better glue, but being able to save lives is a significant advantage. Knowing that scientists are using this research to help find solutions for things as practical as finding victims could further inspire readers to support the preservation of biodiversity.

5. Ecosystems and airplanes both rely on a number of small parts to keep them going. Ecosystems need thousands of species, whereas airplanes need thousands of rivets. Without one or two or even fifteen or twenty rivets or species, both ecosystems and airplanes could still function. Both the rivets and the invertebrates are underappreciated next to larger, more identifiable parts such as wings in the case of airplanes and pandas in the case of ecosystems. What people do not know is how many species can be lost before the ecosystem will collapse, nor exactly how many rivets need to be in place to prevent a plane from crashing. Begley's trying to show that we need these species even if we do not know how much. She wants readers to support biodiversity before the ecosystem falls apart. At that point it will be too late—the system will have crashed, and there will be nothing we can do. We cannot reintroduce something after it is gone, just as you cannot force a crashed plane up into the air.

6. Invertebrates carry the history and information of 99 percent of all animals. We can learn endlessly about the world through them. They provide us with the basis of our knowledge. We need to preserve them the way we

would a precious library. It is our collective knowledge. Libraries might not seem like the most exciting place for many people, but they are inarguably essential.

Classroom Activity Using Writing with Sources

Here are two possible answers for integrating the quotations in the exercise.

1. Most Americans recognize that we are producing more trash per person than ever, that plastic is a huge problem, and that paper biodegrades quickly in landfills. However, Garbage Project director William L. Rathje argues, "The biggest challenge we will face is to recognize that the conventional wisdom about garbage is often wrong" (100).

2. Television, it could be argued, presents life in tidy, almost predictable thirty- and sixty-minute packages. As any episode of *How I Met Your Mother, House,* or *Law and Order* demonstrates, life on television, although exciting, is relatively easy to follow. Humor, simultaneous action, and special effects cannot overshadow that each show has a beginning, a middle, and an end. In contrast, poet Rita Dove writes, "Life . . . is ragged. Loose ends rule" (99). For many Americans, television provides an escape from their disjointed day-to-day lives.

The English-Only Movement: Can America Proscribe Language with a Clear Conscience? (p. 261)
■ Jake Jamieson

Essay Analysis and Discussion

Jamieson challenges the claim that the United States is a melting pot, arguing that many attempts to make people speak English are simply subtle ways to discriminate against immigrants and strip them of their culture. He says that there is no way to melt into one culture because there is no one American way. Just for starters, Americans differ in religion, values, and dress. The various movements to make English the official language in many states exemplify this fact. Jamieson quotes numerous sources both for and against English-only laws. In doing so, he not only supports his claim, but also sets himself up to cite counterarguments.

Thinking Critically about This Reading

Most students will agree that there is at least some variety in American culture. Common language, however, does enable people to be more united. It means that they can access the same information, TV shows, news programs, and jobs, as well as communicate with one another. This shared communication does build certain connections that language barriers maintain. Some students might note that the United States is a younger country than those that many immigrants come from (e.g., China, India) and that it was built by immigrants. There are fewer generations of American-only culture than in nations such as Japan that are unified not only by language, but also by a shared culture developed mostly in isolation.

Questions for Study and Discussion

1. The question Jamieson raises is, "Should immigrants be required to learn English, or should accommodations be made so they can continue to use their native languages?" (paragraph 1). He takes readers through both sides of the argument, citing various sources to argue both points. This balanced view also enables him to make more convincing counterarguments.

2. Jamieson says that the melting pot analogy does not make sense because, in fact, there is no one culture into which immigrants can melt. Americans differ so dramatically from one another that the idea of an "American culture" is hard to defend. There is no shared religion, value structure, or way of dress, which some students may say is what makes the United States appealing. The country encourages people to be individuals and practice their own religions, styles of dress, and values (within certain limits). They are melting into freedom. Other students will agree that the melting pot seems more a popular expression than a reality.

3. English speakers have access to more jobs and can communicate with more Americans. They are therefore more likely to be prosperous, secure, and stable. Without English, many immigrants have limited job opportunities or little opportunity for growth. As a result, attaining the "American Dream"—whether that is a house and two kids or just basic financial security, access to health care, or more opportunities to pursue happiness—is less likely.

4. Lewis's comment takes Dole's a step further. Dole's statement was more idealized and political. Lewis, as a political commentator, speaks more candidly. This contrast allows readers, who may have missed the subtle discrimination Jamieson hopes to demonstrate, to be more attuned to the subtle ways the United States discourages immigrants. Jamieson hopes that readers will see Lewis as less than compassionate and be more open to his next paragraph, which challenges Lewis's way of thinking.

5. According to Crawford, because it is illegal and not politically correct to discriminate based on ethnicity, many people use language as a way to discriminate. They tell immigrants that they must speak English to belong, knowing that many are not able. They can then ostracize them, based on language, and not be criticized for being racist. Crawford would say that Dole's comment exemplifies this racism—suggesting that the "American Dream" is only available to those who speak English. In this way, Dole

45

shuts out the "dream" to many immigrants. Crawford does not believe that we need to encourage the notion that you have to speak English to have financial security and prosperity. The expression of the American Dream for many people brings up images of the 1950s, when everyone knew his or her role in the family and people felt secure. The people in these images are often white. Many people come to the United States for the freedom and economic opportunity and work hard. They, too, Crawford might argue, should be given the same access to prosperity.

6. Jamieson wants to show how these laws are spiraling out of control and how they are being used to discriminate. It seems absurd to most people that speaking only Spanish to your own child would be discrimination. Jamieson makes the point that English-only laws can criminalize being foreign, making the United States the scalding cauldron, rather than the gentle melting pot. In this case, speaking Spanish actually was considered a crime.

7. Jamieson uses signal phrases to introduce quotations, to go deeper into the debate, and to help the reader follow both sides of the argument. In using signal phrases, Jamieson ensures that he will not lose his reader, who will thus clearly understand how each point supports his argument. Otherwise, between having so many sources and all the counterarguments, readers could easily get lost.

8. To the first question he would say that freedom of speech needs to be extended to everyone in the country regardless of the language they speak. To the second, he would argue that everyone deserves to have access to life, liberty, and the pursuit of happiness. To the third, he would want the United States to make sure that we do not just apply this philosophy when it pertains to people "like us."

Classroom Activity Using Writing with Sources

Here is an example of a possible rewrite for the Iyer paragraph:

> Punctuation marks are signs or instructions to the reader. A period says to stop. A comma says to slow down. A semicolon says to pause briefly before beginning again.

Here is an example of a possible rewrite for the Walsh and Burrell paragraph:

> Something that started as no more than a small conflict over salaries for garbage men developed into a large racial fire. The same time that MKL Jr. and members of the SCLC planned a March on Washington in 1968, some garbage men were in a kerfuffle with Tennessee Mayor Henry Loeb. The mostly black garbage men went on strike on February 12th pitting them in a battle; the black union, local 1733, and the historically powerful whites running the City of Memphis.

The Clan of One-Breasted Women (p. 269)
■ Terry Tempest Williams

Essay Analysis and Discussion

This essay is about individuals gathering together and speaking up for themselves using peaceful means. Williams makes the point that her pen is her weapon. She encourages the reader to consider writing as a powerful tool, a tool powerful enough to combat nuclear testing. Have any students in the class written a letter of protest? If so, to whom did they write and for what cause? Do they know whether or not the letter had an effect? Stress the importance of Williams's personal connection to the issue. Her story of her family history makes her writing more powerful than had she simply opposed testing for political reasons.

Thinking Critically about This Reading

Understanding the historical context allows readers to empathize with Williams's courage to speak out. The intensity of the Korean War, McCarthyism, and the fear (and danger) of being called a communist all made speaking out about nuclear testing difficult, scary, and dangerous. Today, Americans know more about the dangers of testing and fear of communist rhetoric has diminished, so speaking out about such matters would more likely be encouraged and supported by the public.

Questions for Study and Discussion

1. Williams begins the essay with the shocking cancer history of her family, reiterating the dramatic title in the first sentence. This beginning account helps readers trust Williams as an authority; she has faced possible cancer and the loss of many family members. Most readers can imagine having the reactions to the testing she describes later; this battle is not an intellectual one for her. Student reactions to this beginning will differ; some may find it off-putting. The intensity of her history may make some students want to stop reading, but others will want to continue.

2. The "new information" her father introduced during dinner was that the recurring dream she thought she had as a child was actually a memory. The "flash of light in the night of the desert" was actually a memory of a bomb they saw being tested in 1957. Williams remarked that this information made her "realize the deceit I had been living under" (paragraph 16). Because of the bombs being tested during her childhood, she had grown up on contaminated land and had consumed contaminated products that would hurt her and kill many women in her family.

3. To support the idea that "public health was secondary to national security," she quotes the Atomic Energy Commissioner saying that nothing

47

would interfere with the tests. The commissioner's use of the word *nothing* implies that even public health would come second.

4. Williams uses a dash to introduce Howard L. Andrews, two commas to introduce his position, and the word *says* to introduce his commentary. Andrews commented on the time required for the body to convert radiation to cancer (14 years). Because her mother's cancer surfaced 14 years after the bomb test in 1957, Williams strengthens her case that her mother's cancer is correlated with the bomb test, especially for those readers who may think that Williams's family cancer comes from a genetic predisposition rather than a result of radiation.

5. Williams remains silent because of her family and religious tradition. She informs the reader that "in Mormon culture, authority is respected, obedience is revered, and independent thinking is not" (30). In addition to a strong cultural tradition that discourages protests, her mother also discouraged speaking up. Her mother told her to let the problem drop, saying that knowing her own feelings was all that mattered. She spoke up only after years of watching the women in her family die and a dream she had of women from all over the world gathering in dance and then protesting with song.

6. Paragraphs 1 through 19 introduce Williams and her family's story; paragraphs 20 through 29 provide the political and historical context; and in paragraphs 30 through 58, Williams describes her own process of overcoming resistance to speak her truth, her powerful dream, and her ultimate approach to instigating change. The three sections interweave Williams's story, with outside context, back to her own personal journey to save herself, her family, and others. She organizes the story this way to first introduce the reader to her situation and then to provide enough outside context and expert testimony to convince the reader to at least entertain the possibility that the cancer is linked to the testimony. Then, finally, she discusses her own personal struggle to free herself (and others) from the cultural, familial, and political pressures to remain silent.

7. The women crossed into the test site to get the attention of the military through an act of civil disobedience. They believed that the only way to stop the devil of radiation was to face it directly. Dancing on the outskirts would do no good. Williams joined them because despite all the pressure to keep quiet, she had made a decision within herself that it was more important to speak her truth and question authority than to receive approval. This trespassing served as a physical demonstration of that decision. Her pen and paper were her weapons because she would write essays such as this one that draw attention to the issue. Her voice, which she had claimed, would be expressed through writing.

Classroom Activity Using Writing with Sources

Review with students the Avoiding Plagiarism box on page 254. Make sure to emphasize that proper paraphrasing expresses the original idea without copying the language and structure of the original writing. Students need to pay close attention to the words they choose, and they must go beyond simply replacing the author's words with their corresponding synonyms.

CHAPTER 11 **Diction and Tone**

Shame (p. 288)
■ **Dick Gregory**

Essay Analysis and Discussion

The heart of this essay is the incident Gregory relates about being shamed in front of Helene Tucker. Gregory chooses a chronological organization, but the chronology does not begin until the fourth paragraph because Gregory needs to establish a context for the incident in paragraphs 1 through 3. To give your students an indication of how vital such a context is to this essay, have them reexamine the first three paragraphs and consider what they contribute to Gregory's narration of the schoolroom incident in paragraphs 4 through 27 and what effect the removal of these three paragraphs would have on the essay. If you wish to narrow the focus of the discussion even further, ask them how the following sentences from those initial paragraphs interact with elements from Gregory's anecdote:

> "It was a lady's handkerchief, but I didn't want Helene to see me wipe my nose on my hand." (paragraph 1)
> "Everybody's got a Helene Tucker, a symbol of everything you want." (2)
> "And she had a Daddy, and he had a good job." (2)
> "When I played the drums in high school it was for Helene and when I broke track records in college it was for Helene and when I started standing behind microphones and heard applause I wished Helene could hear it, too." (3)

After you have discussed the relationship between the opening paragraphs and the episode at school, have students analyze how those three paragraphs connect with Gregory's conclusion. The intent of your discussion should be to clarify what it means to establish a clear context for a narration.

Thinking Critically about This Reading

Gregory, when trying to impress Helene Tucker, told the class that his father would donate 15 dollars to the community chest. His teacher humiliated Gregory by saying that if his father had that much money he did not deserve relief, ultimately silencing Gregory by stating, "We know you don't have a daddy." This rebuke stung Gregory so greatly because he was revealed as a liar in front of the girl whose affection he so desperately wanted.

Questions for Study and Discussion

1. In the first three paragraphs of the essay, Gregory introduces Helene Tucker and tells of his infatuation with her. This information provides the motivation for his later behavior.

2. For Gregory, *shame* means "disgrace," in this case disgrace in an environment where he least expected to find it. Gregory was ashamed of his poverty and of not having a father; however, that day in school was the day "I learned to be ashamed of myself."

3. Students will likely say that Gregory's tone is angry or resigned. Ask students to discuss the meaning of the word *shame* and how Gregory's diction and tone relate that feeling to his audience. Ask students to find words and phrases that relate to cleanliness and dirtiness, or intelligence and stupidity, for example. What do these dualities convey? What do they reveal about Gregory?

4. The teacher thought that Gregory was stupid, he said, but did not stop to consider that he had trouble in school because he was not getting enough to eat at home. She also thought that he was a troublemaker, again not taking time to consider that he was looking for attention he did not get at home. Nevertheless, until the day of his shaming, he thought that she liked him. "She always picked me to wash the blackboard on Friday, after school . . . it made me feel important." Ultimately she showed contempt for "you and your kind," and publicly humiliated him when she announced his secret to the class: "We know you don't have a daddy."

5. This story is not one about racism. In fact, there is nothing to indicate that his teacher was not black. The lack of money is the basis of Gregory's shame, just as it would be having money that erased it. Helene Tucker, the little girl who was light-complexioned, clean, and well-dressed, became the symbol of what he was not. "It wasn't until I was twenty-nine years old and married and making money that I finally got her out of my system."

6. Examples of Gregory's use of descriptive details abound in the essay. (By locating examples, students will become aware of how such details help create vivid and interesting prose.)

7. Although Gregory introduces shame in the first sentence of his first paragraph, the focus of the paragraph is on the "love" (or crush) he has for Helene Tucker. He tells how this "light-complexioned little girl with pigtails and nice manners" made him feel good just being in her company. The final paragraph, in contrast, is dominated by shame. Gregory now felt as if "everyone had heard what the teacher had said, everyone had turned around and felt sorry for me." Gregory effectively uses examples to show how "there was shame everywhere." In a world filled with shame, there is no room for love. Gregory's final paragraph underscores the traumatic effect of the teacher's caustic words and is therefore an emotionally powerful ending.

Classroom Activity Using Diction and Tone

Synonyms for *eat, drink, sleep,* and *work* include the following:

> *eat:* devour, nibble, feast, gorge, gobble, pick, dine, wolf, consume
> *drink:* gulp, quaff, sip, chug, guzzle, imbibe, tipple
> *sleep:* snooze, nap, slumber, doze, catch forty winks, turn in, hit the hay, crash
> *work:* toil, labor, perform, serve, slave, sweat

Make four lists of verbs on the chalkboard. Classroom discussion should focus on the connotative differences between the verbs on each list. Students usually find it helpful to try using each verb in a sentence of their own. Also discuss how the verbs in each list convey more than the meaning contained in *eat, drink, sleep,* and *work.* For example, to *nibble* means to *eat delicately.* Have students translate the verbs on each list. The bottom line is that strong active verbs reduce the need to modify.

Me Talk Pretty One Day (p. 294)
■ David Sedaris

Essay Analysis and Discussion

Sedaris is known for his humorous and ironic essays. In "Me Talk Pretty One Day," Sedaris recounts his experience of taking French language lessons in Paris. His metaphors, similes, and anecdotes make this piece a funny essay, especially if it is read aloud during class. If students have trouble picking up on Sedaris's humorous tone, reading the piece aloud will help them hear the silliness that arises in his classroom. Consider asking students if they have ever been in a situation when they could not communicate effectively, were out of their comfort zone, and at a disadvantage. How did they convey their thoughts? Were they able, in such a situation, to form a sympathetic group camaraderie, as Sedaris does with his classmates?

Thinking Critically about This Reading

That Sedaris can relate—in translation—his French teacher's insult is significant because it shows that he has learned enough of the language to be able to understand her rather obscure barbs. The teacher's cesarean section metaphor illustrates that she sees teaching as a painful process of trying to bring understanding to her students. It also shows that she is as pained by her students as they are by her.

Questions for Study and Discussion

1. Some words and phrases that help Sedaris establish a humorous tone are the following: "true debutant" (paragraph 1), "appears to be a ham sand-

wich" (1), "Pa Kettle trapped backstage after a fashion show" (2), "weave a floor mat out of newspapers" (3), "a failed nursing student to inject me with horse tranquilizer" (3), "teeth the size of tombstones" (9), "Playmate of the Month data sheets" (12), "I love Tums" (15), "severe dermatological conditions" (15), "Lady Flesh Wound or Good Sir Dishrag" (18), "strap on my wooden leg" (23), and "overheard in refugee camps" (25).

2. Students will have different impressions of Sedaris and his classmates. His most striking description of them is of refugees struggling to communicate. Point out to students that the class is filled with a diverse group of people and that they have all come together for a common goal—to learn French.

3. Sedaris uses the jumbled words to illustrate his own inability to fully understand French. Had he included the "real" words instead, his sense of confusion and the drive he felt to learn the language would have been lost.

4. Sedaris's realization is that he can understand his teacher's words. He is able to understand several of her insults and states that "for the first time since arriving in France, I could understand every word that someone was saying."

Classroom Activity Using Diction and Tone

Our students have suggested the following menu descriptions:

tomato juice: spicy tomato juice; tomato juice with a wedge of lemon
onion soup: French onion soup; onion soup covered with cheese and slow-baked in a clay crock
ground beef: Salisbury steak; chopped sirloin smothered with onions and peppers
chicken: tender roasted chicken; lightly breaded, crispy chicken
peas: baby peas; petite farm-fresh peas
potatoes: tender, new potatoes; southern hash brown potatoes
salad: crisp salad greens; fresh garden greens lightly dressed with our house vinaigrette
bread and butter: fresh-baked, whole-grain breads and creamy butter
pasta: fresh, homemade pasta; pasta served al dente
ice cream: creamy gourmet ice cream; premium ice cream
tea: all-natural herb tea; selection of the finest teas from around the world
cake: sinfully delicious triple chocolate cake; delightfully light angel food cake with farm-fresh berries

Try to engage students in a discussion of what the various descriptions tell them about the foods as well as about the restaurants that have these descriptions on their menus. For example, which restaurants serve "hash browns" and which ones serve "tender new potatoes"?

The Center of the Universe (p. 302)
■ **Tina McElroy Ansa**

Essay Analysis and Discussion

This essay demonstrates how our perceptions can change over time. As a child, Ansa thought that Georgia was the center of the universe. As she grew up, she learned that the Georgia that raised her was just one place in time and space. In paragraph 16, Ansa says, "Like all of us, I carry my childhood with me." Do students believe that they carry their childhood with them? Ask them to think of people in their family who never talk about their childhood or about whose childhood they know little. Do they think that everybody so consciously carries their childhood like Ansa? Why or why not? In what ways could the process of writing keep one's childhood alive? Writing can be a way of staying in touch with one's childhood.

Thinking Critically about This Reading

Some people might find Ansa's talk about loving the South uncomfortable because it's hard for some to understand why an African American woman would love a region with such a tragic history of slavery and segregation. African Americans came to the South against their will, as slaves; so calling herself a proud Southerner might sound tantamount to saying that she's glad her ancestors were brutally treated. When she spent time up north, however, she realized that she did not feel at home there. This realization helped clarify for her that, yes, she *is* a southerner. You may want to ask students how the essay might differ if Ansa had visited the African country from whence her ancestors were taken and still felt more like a southerner. How would this approach have been more or less powerful?

Questions for Study and Discussion

As a child, the meaning to Ansa was that *she* was at the center of the universe.

1. She organizes the essay by first talking about her childhood perception of Georgia as the center of the universe; she then introduces her thesis about being proud to be a southerner, explains her family history, and shares with the reader the stories of her family that made her fall in love with the region so that the reader could understand her feelings and perhaps even find some love for the region.
2. Student answers will vary. Because Ansa talks a great deal about her loving memories of the south, many students will say that the essay sounds nostalgic. Although she takes herself seriously, Ansa's informal and welcoming tone invites the reader into her family, sharing with us the smallest details of her family life (like the barber chair on the family porch).

3. Ansa discusses her great-auntie often in the essay, but students will have to infer why she is so important and what role she had on Ansa's life. Ansa writes atop the Singer sewing machine table that was in her aunt's bedroom. Students may notice that her aunt seems to be the strong support under her writing, the solid four legs and tabletop that give her strength. Her aunt had strong beliefs about right and wrong and a strong sense of purpose. She taught people how to read, meaning that she valued reading. This focus on reading might have inspired Ansa, a future writer. As a child, Ansa saw her aunt only as "stern"; as an adult, she saw her as extraordinary. Ansa's aunt believed in hard, sober (no Coca-Cola or aspirin) work. Ansa could arguably have been inspired by this woman to stick by her own beliefs (being a proud southerner makes sense), to work hard, and to write.

4. When Ansa had the phonebook she would look up friends' phone numbers and imagine the lives of people she did not know. For an aspiring writer, it provided practice creating characters and stories.

5. Ansa says she draws "sustenance from these stories" (paragraph 14). The stories she overheard wove the context of her life. The stories taught her about life, love, and the inner worlds of the people she saw coming and going in her life. Students will be affected differently by the stories. Some will be touched by her aunt's funny commitment to visiting the Holy Land but refusing to cross water, some by the mother's loving cooking, and others by the family's landowning farmers.

6. Again, students will have different opinions about the ending. Readers may wonder why, if Ansa loves it so much, she no longer lives there. They might find that it weakens her argument even though she claims hat she has the town within her. Others may relate to the idea that a place, like childhood, resides within us, meaning that you never really have to leave.

Classroom Activity Using Diction and Tone

humorous: silly, surprising, ironic, giggle
angry: hot-headed, upset, yell, scream
authoritative: controlling, knowledgeable, experienced
triumphant: glorious, winning, overcome obstacles
tentative: unsure, confused, hesitant
repentant: regretful, forgiveness, religion

Irreconcilable Dissonance (p. 308)
■ **Brian Doyle**

Essay Analysis and Discussion

Doyle here collects and shares reasons that people give for why they decided to get divorced. The examples he selects seem so extreme that they border on the absurd. Surely in each case, the stated reason is not the only reason, or the stated reason stands emblematically for a larger problem or incompatibility, but Doyle's litany of odd reasons for divorce successfully conveys that divorce is common and a possible option always hovering between two married people. Because it is undertaken for all kinds of reasons, no one in a marriage is ever truly safe from it, Doyle seems to be saying. Discuss with students how his approach—of listing unusual, far-fetched stated reasons—serves Doyle's purpose. With these examples, he can set his tone (conveying a sense of wonder that anyone stays together) and muse on how staying together takes day-to-day, minute-to-minute, flexible forbearance and an acceptance of "the shagginess of things" (paragraph 8). Ask students if they know of other divorce examples. In other words, in their lives what reasons for divorce have they heard? What conclusions have they drawn about marriage and divorce? What "tricks" or coping strategies have they observed that people use to stay together, given the challenges inherent in long-term relationships?

Thinking Critically about This Reading

Student answers will vary. Those who seek adventure and variety may understand how the monotony of an unchanging daily life can make one want to make a drastic change. Those who do not like change, who like the comfort of the mundane, may share Doyle's "willies." Some students might answer the second part of this question by saying that those getting married must commit to working through the "shifting expectations and external parade of small surprises." The only safe place to stand is at the altar (metaphorically), the place of commitment. Doyle believes that living with the constant knowledge that the marriage could dissolve at any minute is the only safe place to stand.

Questions for Study and Discussion

1. Students may note that the long first sentence sets the tone for the essay. Doyle brings the reader into what sounds more like an internal dialogue than a formal introduction to an essay. The first and last paragraphs both use the phrase that "every marriage is pregnant with divorce" and discuss that idea.
2. Some reasons for divorce were the following: one man wanted to watch a TV show from start to finish, another wanted to fart in peace, and another for no reason other than he did not want to be married anymore. Then came the more standard reason—the woman fell in love with another man—followed by the less standard reason—a woman leaving a man right after the man mimicked a dog peeing on a hydrant. Because most of these reasons seem like such arbitrary excuses to divorce, Doyle chalks them up to the "chaotic wilderness of human nature." They seem random and illogical.
3. What shocked Doyle about the first divorce he saw is that he seems to have seen the beginning, when they still loved each other, declared that love in

front of others, and even had a child. Seeing a couple make such a complete turnabout really struck him. What keeps him thinking about that first divorce is having seen how good could so quickly turn into something so terrible.

4. Doyle was fascinated by "irresolute differences" and "irreconcilable dissonances" as grounds for divorce because the words express exactly and precisely the reality. In Doyle's words, "the exact right words are applied to the exact right reason for those words" (paragraph 6).

5. Student answers will vary. Many, however, may say that Doyle is humorous, informal, and a bit flip. Others may say he is irreverent, cynical, quirky, or bemused. The words *mivorced, darried, sleeperated,* and *schleperated* add levity and playfulness to his article. Other words that keep the essay light are *fart* (2), *puppylike* (6), *shagginess* (8), and *garden gnome* (9). Doyle's playful tone concerning a topic that causes many people enormous pain allows people to laugh at themselves rather than create more drama and, perhaps, ultimately in laughing find ways to stay together.

6. Doyle, having married and stayed married, presumably values marriage and is willing to see through the ups and downs. His article seems to mock the people who marry (and divorce) more than the institution itself. The "chaotic wilderness of human nature" makes the institution of marriage difficult to maintain, not because it demands the extraordinary, but because it forces people to face the ordinary, together. The numerous ridiculous reasons he has cited for divorce suggests that he believes that most people are better off staying married than throwing everything away for a 24-hour *Wire* marathon.

Classroom Activity Using Diction and Tone

Doyle's advice is filled with directives or commands, such as "write," "never," "live," "carry," and "don't." His clear dos and don'ts written in short sentences sets the tone. He sounds like a football coach. The tone lacks ambiguity and gives students clear guidelines in the often uncertain world of writing. Many will enjoy this direct, strict, and yet positive approach.

CHAPTER 12 **Figurative Language**

The Barrio (p. 316)
■ **Robert Ramirez**

Essay Analysis and Discussion

Ramirez points out the sights of the barrio from a moving train that emerges in the "deep sleep" of night in the opening paragraph and reappears to the "yawns and restless stretchings" of a new dawn in the closing paragraph. Students can discuss this use of figurative language in asking four questions: Why does Ramirez use a train to establish a context for his description of the barrio? Why does he take us into the barrio only through the still hours of the night? What does he intend as the symbolism of the train and the street lamp? What do they add to his portrayal of the barrio?

Thinking Critically about This Reading

Ramirez goes on to say, "The barrio is a refuge from the harshness and the coldness of the Anglo world. It is a forced refuge" (paragraph 4). In paragraphs 5 through 10, he describes the institutions of the barrio and their importance in the community: the *tortillería, panadería,* corner grocery store, barbershop, pool hall, and *cantina.* These examples support his claim that the barrio is more than a home by illustrating that it is also a protected zone of culture, community, and family.

Questions for Study and Discussion

1. *Barrio* is a Spanish word that refers to a chiefly Spanish-speaking neighborhood (typically in a city) in the southwestern United States. Ramirez generally describes barrios as isolated communities "fenced off by railroads, canals, and expressways" (2). Because the barrio is a "refuge from the harshness and the coldness of the Anglo world" (4), members of the barrio have no desire to leave. All their needs are met within its confines.

2. The Spanish phrases, spoken as if the reader understands them, lend an aura of authenticity and color to Ramirez's essay. These words allow us to "hear" the people of the barrio. The other words connote warmth, community, intimacy, and friendliness. They are meant to emphasize the positive feelings of life in the barrio that are known only to its inhabitants.

3. "[T]his pulsing light . . . beats slower, like a weary heartbeat" (1). "[F]rom the angry seeds of rejection grow the flowers of closeness between outcasts, not the thorns of bitterness" (4). "[T]he warmth of the tortilla factory is a wool *sarape*" (5). "Their houses, aged and bent, oozing children, are fissures in the horn of plenty" (17). These metaphors are particularly apt because they compare things common to the barrio with other things that are relevant to it. The wool *sarape* is as common as the factory. The horn of plenty, broken and empty, is also a metaphor for the people of the barrio.

4. Ramirez uses a number of words and phrases that attribute human characteristics to the barrio and the daily train. They include "blinks" (1), "pulsing" (1), "weary heartbeat" (1), "grumble" (2), "arrest" (13), "ignore" (13), and "greets a new dawn with yawns and restless stretchings" (20).

5. Ramirez intends his comparison of the fences in the barrio with the walls of the Anglo community to symbolize the easy interaction among the people of his culture as opposed to the isolation and separation of the Anglo world.

6. Had Ramirez begun his description of the barrio with the negative aspects of life there, he would have risked having readers misunderstand the intent of his essay. Ramirez wants us to understand that life in the barrio is integral, satisfying, and necessary. He saves the sadder aspects of barrio life until the end so that we do not confuse his desire for our understanding with a desire for pity.

Classroom Activity Using Figurative Language

Possible metaphors or similes for each of the items on the list include:

1. *skyscraper:* huge glass needle
2. *sound of an explosion:* rumble of distant thunder, cannon shot
3. *intelligent student:* computer
4. *crowded bus:* stuffed turkey, packed suitcase
5. *slow-moving car:* snail, turtle, tank
6. *pillow:* puffy cloud, flat pancake
7. *narrow alley:* cave, tunnel
8. *greasy french fries:* slippery carrot sticks, glistening wet skin
9. *hot sun:* roasting oven, baking, sear like a flame
10. *dull knife:* cutting with wooden utensil, frustrating as playing golf with the wrong club

Engage students in a discussion of the various figures of speech that they came up with for each item, and have them decide which ones work best. They will see that good figures of speech are those that are fresh (not clichéd) and create a clear mental image.

Polaroids (p. 323)
■ Anne Lamott

Essay Analysis and Discussion

Ideally, bring in a Polaroid camera or ask a student to bring one in. It is possible at this point that some students may not have seen a Polaroid photo develop. The lesson will be more powerful with an example, especially a photo of the class. Often writers say that the story began to have a life of its own or that certain characters showed up unexpectedly. This "coming to life" can happen in fiction writing, authors say. Characters can "introduce themselves" and take major roles in the story, much to the surprise of the author. Ask students if they have ever met someone, thinking that he or she was just going to be an acquaintance or less and instead ended up playing a more major role in their lives.

Thinking Critically about This Reading

The pride that the African American man takes in himself reveals to Lamott her theme of a struggle and tragedy transformed to joy and triumph.

Questions for Study and Discussion

1. The analogy is that the process of writing is like the developing of a Polaroid picture. There is a gradual emergence and clarification of the Polaroid, and the result might look different from what was expected. Lamott is writing about writing, of course, and the Polaroid analogy helps her explain the way she views how a piece of writing develops.

2. Students will choose different examples. One metaphor is "the shadows begin to appear, and then you start to see the animal tragedy" (paragraph 1), which communicates what happens when you get deeper into a subject and you start to see the profound and disturbing. Lamott uses the simile "thick and slow as a warped record" (8) to describe the African American man's impaired speech. Figures of speech make these imaginative connections that surprise readers. Similarly, first drafts often create surprises for writers.

3. The "grayish green murk" is the void from which the image emerges in a Polaroid, and Lamott repeats the words (1, 10) to emphasize the importance of the murk to the analogy. To a photographer, it is a literal murk, in which chemicals and light exposure react to make an image. To a writer, it is a metaphorical murk of thoughts and subject matter that eventually produces coherent meaning.

4. The four unexpected elements in the Polaroid are family, shadows, red flowers, and props. They represent the thoughts and memories that do not emerge in one's mind until after one starts writing about a subject in a first draft.

5. In describing the Special Olympics as she did, Lamott shows the reader an example of the writer's Polaroid process. In other words, she describes "the picture she is seeing" at the Olympics, and little by little the story starts to come into focus, more characters appear, and the scene comes into vision. By the end of the section, readers can clearly picture the event. This example allows her to unify the essay by not only telling the reader about how watching a Polaroid coming focus is like writing, but also by showing the reader.

Classroom Activity Using Figurative Language

Student reactions to the essays will differ. Several examples of figures of speech from each essay are listed below.

In "The Fading Season," the author used *personification* as the predominant figure of speech:

- "spilled in scarlet syllables" (1)
- "fluttering leaflets bear bittersweet messages" (2)
- "in the fingers of slim sunbeams" (2)
- "the earth before it dozes off for another winter" (3)

In "October," the author also used *personification* as the predominant figure of speech:

- "comes striding over the hills wearing a crimson shirt" (1)
- "His morning breath" (1)
- "a god of travel" (2)
- "it is full of lively spirit" (3)
- "you can hear October, that fellow in the crimson shirt, whistling a soft melody that is as old as autumn upon this earth" (3)
- Whistling a soft medley (3)

Invasion (p. 329)
■ Benjamin Percy

Essay Analysis and Discussion

Some students may react to Percy's violent way of handling the insects. He killed them in brutal ways. As an adult, with newcomers he was less outwardly hostile, but still dismayed. In what ways were Percy's childhood antics more in line with the more bestial side of humans? Regarding his distaste for newcomers, discuss with the class one's natural instinct to protect one's home. Ask students for examples of people in their lives who refer to towns, universities, parks, and so forth that they claim were better before newcomers arrived. Is there a natural instinct to resist change? People critique gentrification as much as they critique dilapidation.

Thinking Critically about This Reading

As a young person growing up in Bend, Oregon, Percy would have also seen himself as someone belonging to Bend versus owning the land. He hunted and lived off its animals, rode through its forests, and worked with the soil's impoverished condition. This background, too, explains why he defended the land as he did. Also, he may have deeply related to the Suquamish Indians' deep desire to protect their land from those who sought to dominate it. Percy's family worked *with* the land, irrigating it and living within it. The newcomers just added paved roads and chain stores where acres of sagebrush used to cover the landscape. They dominated versus lived within the land, as did Percy and his family.

Questions for Study and Discussion

1. The dominant impression of the Bend, Oregon, that Percy grew up in is a rugged and unpretentious town filled with laborers, farmers, and self-reliant country people happy with their way of life and uninterested in the ways of others.

2. Percy's purpose is to show how his town has changed, pointing out to wealthy people how they may look to original townspeople. He expects readers to consider and respect, if they move into older communities, the way of life that preceded their arrival and the effect their arrival has on others.

3. Figurative language offers people a new way of looking at the world and is not to be taken literally, such as when Percy describes a melting mailbox resembling a dying trout. In this case, turning a plastic mailbox into a regional animal, he shows his attempts to exchange the "plastic" people for the local fauna. He also used figurative language via the simile of a work-glove to describe the skin of their fathers. His use of the caterpillar and moth analogy is the primary use of figurative language.

4. Percy uses the analogy of the Pandora moth epidemic. The newcomers arrive like the moth while he and his friends do everything they can to kill the caterpillars with their bike tires and kill the moths with tennis rackets and their cars. Students might also liken Percy's time in Bend as the caterpillar stage, not pretty or fancy but close to the land. The newcomers, mostly from California, serve as the moths, flying about disconnected from the stage that came before them and oblivious to the land beneath their wings. They are not as beautiful as butterflies, but are freer than caterpillars. Student opinions about the effectiveness of the analogy will vary. Many will probably enjoy the image of Percy going after the rich newcomers and a kid squashing a caterpillar.

5. Percy uses a straightforward and objective style when he cites the population growth in Bend, Oregon. This objective style helps the reader understand the size of the regional shift, rather than simply Percy's reaction to the change. When he talks about the kinds of stores the newcomers brought (wine shops, clothing boutiques, white-linen restaurants), the brands they wore, and the cars they drove, readers have a clear idea of the nature of the shift. In addition, quoting the governor and the billboards in a straightforward way shows the reader that Percy's reaction was that of simply a rebellious young man and his friends. Many others in the whole region shared the sentiment about newcomers.

6. In the final paragraph, Percy realizes that the town no longer belongs to him. He sees the newcomers as moths and his era as the caterpillars. He, his era, and the land are simply shaken off the newcomers as a moth would shake dust off its wings.

Classroom Activity Using Figurative Language

Break into small groups and have each writer read his or her writing to the group. The group, after listening, is to jot down the words, phrases, or points that were most powerful. Then the group shares their comments. The writer will learn what others perceive as effective and whether the group agrees as a whole. It is better not to have the group make notes while the writer is reading because it may influence other group members. If the images are compelling, they will remember, and it will force them to listen carefully.

CHAPTER 13 **Illustration**

A Crime of Compassion (p. 343)
■ **Barbara Huttmann**

Essay Analysis and Discussion

At the heart of Huttmann's dramatic and often shocking essay is the story of her young patient. In the beginning of her essay we meet him, a strong, confident, healthy young man. Then Huttmann proceeds in a chronological order to describe the rapid deterioration that ends in his death. Other things are happening as well: the collapse of his family and the nurse's own evolution from rule-abiding health worker to mercy "killer." Yet as dramatic as Huttmann's tale is, it remains a model of "show, don't tell." For Huttmann never asks us to weep — she moves us to tears with the details of the events she witnessed and the emotions she experienced. Even those who condemn her actions would be hard pressed to remain unmoved by the horrors the young family experienced. Ask students to reread Huttmann's essay carefully to see how she sustains the dramatic atmosphere of her story. Which kinds of evidence were convincing, and which were not? In the end, is she successful in convincing readers of the justness of her actions?

Thinking Critically about This Reading

Huttmann puts the word *life* in quotation marks to emphasize that the life her patient Mac was living was not one he wished to live. This emphasis also points to her argument that in situations like Mac's there really isn't a simple definition for life. Is it simply brain activity and respiration, or is there a question of quality and intent?

Questions for Study and Discussion

1. Huttmann did not have the legal right to end her patient's life. By that definition, she is a murderer. However, her defenders no doubt will point out that the definition of murder as the premeditated and malicious killing of a human being does not fit the circumstances of Huttmann's deed. She killed out of love, not hate, and the decision to do so was painful, given her attitude that life is something that must be sustained and nurtured. As Huttmann wondered at the right of doctors to sustain life beyond reasonable bounds, she no doubt questioned their right, and hers, to end it. That is why she argues so strenuously for a patient's right to make this terrible decision.

2. Huttmann's essay is as much a tale of her own struggle as it is the story of her patient's decline and death. She begins in paragraph 7 by telling us how often Mac had to be resuscitated and the terrible and grisly agony he went through. By paragraph 8, she is praying he will die, but she has not yet thought of helping him to do it. In paragraph 9, she asks for a "no-code order," which only a doctor can issue. In other words, it is not illegal for doctors to allow a patient to die, only for a nurse to do so. When her request was refused, she contemplated the implications of failing to press the button. By paragraph 10, when Mac had undergone 52 codes, she began appealing to a higher court, a spiritual judge to question the necessity of her actions. She began to be haunted by the question that modern technology has made inevitable: Do we have the right to play God, not in taking life, but in sustaining it beyond all hope? Finally, she makes us witness her panic and fear as she makes the decision *not* to press the button. Her story is compelling and terrifying, and she spares us little of the terror she experienced in making her final decision.

3. As Huttmann explains in paragraph 18, a doctor may legally issue a no-code order. The hypocrisy for her is that the charge of murder is based not on intent but on which uniform a person wears.

4. In paragraph 7, Huttmann describes the work a team of nurses had to do over Mac's body: "The nurses stayed to wipe the saliva that drooled from his mouth, irrigate the big craters of bedsores that covered his hips, suction the lung fluids that threatened to drown him, clean the feces that burned his skin like lye, pour the liquid food down the tube attached to his stomach, put pillows between his knees to ease the bone-on-bone pain, turn him every hour to keep the bedsores from getting worse, and change his gown and linen every two hours to keep him from being soaked in perspiration." Such graphic descriptions are necessary to force the reader to see what Huttmann saw and, however feebly, to feel what Mac felt. She knows that it is easy to make philosophical decisions about life and death from a distance. She wants to rub the readers' noses in the truth.

5. As her essay moves forward, Huttmann intensifies the story by going into lengthier detail about shorter periods of time. No doubt this approach is meant to parallel as much as possible the way in which Mac's pain escalated, not only in intensity but in the horror of its detail.

6. Quite simply, Huttmann means to say that as long as medical science and its practitioners have the means to keep patients alive and believe that they must do so, and as long as the decision not to resuscitate rests with the doctors, patients cannot legally choose to die.

Classroom Activity Using Illustration

This exercise has worked well in getting students to see the relationship between a thesis statement and what is necessary to make it credible and convincing. Of course, this exercise can also be used to have students generate a series of shorter examples, but here the focus is on the single example, which allows for some degree of depth and detail. You may want to have students think about possible examples and also compose one.

- Friends can be welcome and handy to have. (*Possible example:* You need to move large furniture and cannot pay for professional movers.)
- Having good study skills can improve a student's grades (*Possible example:* A student creates a new habit of reviewing his daily class notes right before bed and finds that his grades improved.)
- Loud music can damage your hearing. (*Possible example:* A good friend works on a rock concert tour and loses part of her hearing.)
- Reading the directions for a new product you have just purchased can save time and aggravation. (*Possible example:* Someone struggles hours on Photoshop and then decides to take the 20-minute tutorial included in the program and completes the whole task within an hour.)
- Humor can often make a bad situation more tolerable. (*Possible example:* Some doctors, like Patch Adams, kept patients' spirits up by wearing a clown nose and making jokes.)
- U.S. manufacturers can make their products safer. (*Possible example:* Some car company rebuilt their automobiles to ensure that children cannot open the doors from the inside.)

Let's Think Outside the Box of Bad Clichés (p. 349)
■ Gregory Pence

Essay Analysis and Discussion

Pence lists the variety of clichés he finds in both student papers and professional writing. From "it goes without saying" (paragraph 2) to "it's not for me to say" (2), most readers will be familiar with Pence's examples and reflect on their own use of prefabricated phrases. Pence claims that clear writing is clear thinking. Students may argue in defense of some of the phrases, finding them charming. "It's raining cats and dogs" and "he won by a landslide" could be seen as charming ways to describe the ordinary.

Thinking Critically about This Reading

Pence would agree with Orwell. Both argue that rather than provide readers with something that opens them up, many writers rely on standard expressions. Lost are an appreciation of words and a freshness of prose. Pence alludes to not using clichés requiring more work. Finding a fresh way to express something requires thinking. You may want to ask students why they think that they use standard expressions. Do they do it because they think that readers will relate better or because they can't think of a better way to communicate an idea? Are clichés laziness in writing?

Questions for Study and Discussion

1. Pence's thesis is that students rely on "many trite or inaccurate phrases" to make a point (1). His long lists of clichés used by students and professional writers and within various disciplines demonstrates to the reader how often we rely on well-known phrases. He gives a wide-enough breadth of examples to connect with most readers, who might find themselves guilty of one or two examples. Most students will say he proved his thesis.

2. Pence cites phrases used in college essays and colloquial conversations, and within various industries. Some of the expressions used in the essays, such as "who can say?" (3) or "it's not for me to say" (2), weaken the students' arguments. Such clichés weaken the writer's authority. If the writer believes that he or she is not authorized to make a claim, why should a reader listen? Redundant expressions also hurt an author's authority because they make him or her look uneducated, as in the examples "mass exodus" (5) and "dead carcass" (11). Educated readers will know that the author has not mastered the meanings of these nouns. "Raining cats and dogs" is just silly rather than harmful. No reader takes it literally. One could argue that finding a new expression for a downpour would result in more interesting reading. Some students may say that clichés can be useful when they ensure that readers will truly understand an author's meaning. Because they are known expressions, readers will not misinterpret their meanings. Pence would probably say that there are no good clichés.

3. In the medical example, Pence uses two clichés: "the patient was declared brain dead" and "life support was removed" (8). For many people, these statements create confusion, begging the question "When did he actually die?" To eliminate this confusion, Pence rewrote the paragraph to clarify that "brain dead" is the neurological criteria by which doctors determine that someone is dead. This description clarifies for nonmedical readers that brain activity rather than respiration can be the determining factor when declaring someone dead or alive.

4. Pence explained that he found clichés by going through students' writing and looking for them. Students can reread their own writing and underline any expressions they think might be clichés and then to go back and replace those prefabricated phrases with their own words. Another approach is to read an essay aloud to a friend and see if either that person or the writer can pick out the clichés. You could tell students to think of using clichés as cultural plagiarism—stealing expressions from the culture rather than using their own minds to come up with original phrasing.

5. To end his essay, Pence strung together a list of clichés to reinforce his point that these expressions replace the work of the writer and look silly to readers.

He could have ended his essay by refusing to use any clichés and showing instead the benefits of active and intelligent original prose.

Classroom Activity Using Illustration

Completing the expressions:

> when push comes to shove
> fall between the cracks
> scratch the surface
> paying lip service
> put the cart before the horse
> patience of a saint

Our Vanishing Night (p. 355)
■ Verlyn Klinkenborg

Essay Analysis and Discussion

Klinkenborg presents a solid analysis of light pollution. He provides numerous examples and concrete solutions. His tone and diction are all reasoned. Point out to students or ask them to notice that all the paragraphs are roughly the same length. Ask them how a reasoned approach helps Klinkenborg illustrate his point. Ask them to consider how he could have illustrated his point in a more radical way. How would a more radical illustration of his point have affected the readers? For example, if he had described, in detail, the tragic results of light pollution, he may have come off as a radical and lost the attention of some of his readers.

Thinking Critically about This Reading

The only benefit to lighting up the night in Klinkenborg's essay could be for the pipistrelle bats, which feed off of the bugs on the lamps. Otherwise, he discusses no positive aspects. The consequences are many, but are most powerfully stated in his conclusion, "we have cut ourselves off from our evolutionary and cultural patrimony" (14). This action affects not only humans, but also a variety of other creatures, including birds, turtles, and bats. Migration, mating, and hunting patterns have all been affected.

Questions for Study and Discussion

1. Klinkenborg presents his thesis in paragraph 2: "Ill-designed lighting washes out the darkness of night and radically alters the light levels—and light rhythms—to which many forms of life, including ourselves, have adapted."

2. Klinkenborg includes the following examples of light pollution: the light generated by a fishing fleet can be seen from outer space (paragraph 4), and in most major cities you cannot see the stars (5). In paragraphs 6 through 9, he goes on to give multiple examples on the "effects" of light pollution on the behavior of a variety of animals, including songbirds, sea turtles, and bats. Students will provide the examples that were most meaningful to them.

3. Diurnal creatures have "eyes adapted to living in the sun's light" (1).

4. Light is such a powerful biological force that birds have been known to circle around gas flares and searchlights to their death. The pull of light was stronger than their survival instinct.

5. In paragraph 10, Klinkenborg suggests reengineering lighting to lessen pollution: "Simple changes in lighting design and installation yield immediate changes in the amount of light spilled into the atmosphere and, often, immediate energy savings."

6. Because light has such a powerful effect on the mating, migration, and feeding patterns of animals, it surely has an effect on humans. He would like to see us as part of the natural cycle of day and night rather than manipulating it. Because of light pollution, those living in cities can rarely see the stars and remember that they are part of a larger universe. Students will agree and disagree with this argument. Some may say that medicine, too, could be argued as going against nature, as could agriculture. Others may agree and believe that humans would be better off without so much light at night. Because the world's most populous and intelligent species is diurnal, to some it might make sense that humans would try to adapt the environment to meet their needs.

Classroom Activity Using Illustration

Student opinions will vary. Generalizations would allow the reader to always exclude himself or herself. By listing a variety of specific items, most readers will identify with at least one item and ask themselves whether that item really *is* necessary. To encourage all readers to consider their habit of carrying around so much, Weeks wants to cast the widest net possible. He lists specific items such as cell phones, coffee cups, Gatorade jugs, laptops, and iPods, all things that many students find themselves carrying every day.

You may want to ask students if they agree with Weeks's conclusion—that these belongings are burdens rather than assets. Some students may disagree with his conclusion and say that although they are carrying more stuff, they are also more entertained and occupied. Regardless, students can see the advantage of using specific examples to make a point. Whether or not they agree with it, the examples Weeks provides, rather than generalizations, clearly support his conclusions.

In Defense of Dangerous Ideas (p. 361)
■ **Steven Pinker**

Essay Analysis and Discussion

Pinker challenges readers by showing numerous examples of ideas society would often deem too dangerous to discuss. In so doing, he not only catches the attention of the reader, he reopens these issues for discussion. Rather than diving more deeply into the ideas presented, Pinker wants to encourage readers to dive more deeply themselves into all cultural ideas that may be considered dangerous. He distinguishes between dangerous ideas and ideas that promote evil ideologies or mass destruction. He means ideas that are thought to "corrode the prevailing moral order" (paragraph 24). His generous use of examples helps readers immediately identify the types of ideas he plans to discuss and their overall effect.

Thinking Critically about This Reading

Pinker wants people to be more open to discussing ideas that might not be politically correct, but could be culturally important. He fears that we stop our own cultural growth and ability to improve when we find certain ideas, no matter how important, too dangerous to discuss. Pinker hopes that after reading this essay, readers will think about the ideas he presented and be open to such ideas the next time they encounter one. Instead of quickly dismissing such ideas as too dangerous, he wants readers to entertain and explore these ideas. Some students may be more convinced by his counterarguments than by his defense of dangerous ideas. Some will feel excited by this opportunity to discuss topics previously seen as taboo, since young people are notoriously interested in topics considered taboo by their parents and society. Often young people have the passion and energy to push conversations forward.

Questions for Study and Discussion

1. Students may react differently to the ideas depending on their race, gender, religion, background, and political views. When reading the list, many students may be considering the cultural implications of these ideas if proven true. They also may be stimulated by these ideas because they have wondered about them themselves or have never felt permitted to think about these topics in such a direct way.
2. Pinker defines dangerous ideas as "ideas that are denounced not because they are self-evidently false, nor because they advocate harmful action, but because they are thought to corrode the prevailing moral order" (24). Some students may not agree that these ideas are dangerous, so much as they are considered politically incorrect. Others may find these ideas morally reprehensible.

3. In paragraph 27, Pinker reminds readers of the fear people have historically felt concerning the structure of the solar system. He talks about the fear that has created "moral panic" (25) throughout time, in regard to both geocentrism and evolution. Today, questions about the environment may be considered dangerous. The other factors making an idea "dangerous" have to do with the possible implications of the idea. For example, if women generally have less aptitude in science, will they be less encouraged to pursue a career in science, or will schools stop educating women in science? If people stopped believing in the literal truth of the Bible, would they also put aside the Ten Commandments (29)? People fear that the outcome would be the promotion or encouragement of racism, sexism, and so forth.

4. Student opinions will vary regarding Pinker's claim that some ideas could be considered taboo in the context of personal relationships. Some will have a hard time segmenting ideas into these categories. Why can't you discuss dangerous ideas in some areas of your life if they are acceptable in others? When running a country or discovering how the world works, the only way to progress is to seek the truth. A country cannot be run well without asking tough questions; nor can scientific truths be illuminated without unimpeded inquiry. A personal relationship can function and thrive without this pursuit.

5. To not consider whether an idea has merit is antithetical to the nature of ideas. Humans have ideas. By definition, an idea has to be considered. An idea is born or created solely for that purpose. Ideas come from the consolidation of bits of information, and to not even entertain their worth is to go against the brain and the genius of humankind. One does not have to pursue ideas, but to deny them outright is antilife.

6. Pinker does provide some solid counterarguments claiming that yes, the world is full of malevolent people who will use the vehicles of science and inquiry to justify their racist or destructive views. Also, once the wider public is introduced to a "dangerous idea," the idea gains some power of its own. People might feel the need to act on their suspicion of racial or gender differences if certain studies suggest these biases have some merit. Even if intellectuals try to prevent this type of biased action, masses notoriously oversimplify hypotheses and scientific outcomes. Also, although we are rational beings, sometimes we stop short of seeking the whole truth. For various reasons, people may leave a topic half-explored, allowing certain biases and incorrect conclusions to persist.

7. Pinker cites a book by Alan Kors and Harvey Silverglate, *The Shadow University,* and another by Morton Hunt, *The New Know-Nothings,* which discuss how universities have failed to defend those who have spoken out and acted on their freedom of inquiry and expression. Universities are supposed to protect the freedom of inquiry, hence the invention of tenure. Sadly, it is often the intervention of courts rather than universities that

ensures this protection. In many cases, these rights are not defended at all. Chris Mooney writes about how legislators increasingly stop research that gets in the way of their interests.

Classroom Activity Using Illustration

Students will come up with a host of fad diets, and they will easily engage in a discussion of their examples. Be sure to ask students how their examples illustrate the claim in the topic sentence, which posits that Americans are obsessed with thinness, sometimes to extremes.

CHAPTER 14 **Narration**

What's in a Name? (p. 376)
■ **Henry Louis Gates Jr.**

Essay Analysis and Discussion

When examining this essay with students, have them notice the vital role dialogue plays in it once Gates arrives at the encounter between Mr. Wilson and Gates's father. Consider, in particular, the juxtaposition of the conversation Gates has with his father about why Mr. Wilson calls him "George" with the bit of dialogue that would spring up to break painful moments of silence when the adults in Gates's life were forced to acknowledge "one of those things." The first example of dialogue highlights the innocence with which Gates, the child, confronts a moment of racial awareness, while the second displays the more subtle, more sophisticated manner in which adults deal with similar moments.

Thinking Critically about This Reading

Gates's phrase "one of those things" refers to acts of prejudice and racism that African Americans face on a regular basis. It reflects Gates's purpose for his own story because such acts represent "a world that we could not affect but that affected us" (paragraph 12). He could not alter Mr. Wilson's attitude, yet that attitude affected Gates significantly, as evidenced by his never again looking Mr. Wilson in the eye. Students' opinions on what the final statement means may vary, some believing that it reflects Gates's resentment at Mr. Wilson's racist attitude, others seeing it as representative of Gates's diminished sense of self, knowing that Mr. Wilson views African Americans with contempt.

Questions for Study and Discussion

1. Students' views on the two opening quotations may vary considerably. Gates wishes to highlight how African Americans have been labeled, usu-

ally in a derogatory manner, while also recognizing the effect of such labels on self-identity among African Americans. Both quotations therefore connect with how Gates's experience hearing his father referred to as "George" affected his own sense of self.

2. Here, too, students may have differing views on Gates's reference to Trey Ellis's *Village Voice* essay. The key to their responses, however, may lie in how Gates frames the reference within the discovery that he had forgotten all about the incident when his father was called "George" until he read Ellis's essay. Chances are students will recognize the way in which the things they read often trigger similar kinds of reminiscences. Whether they can envision themselves using such an opening approach in their own writing may depend, to some extent, on the amount and type of reading they do. One side benefit of Gates's allusion is that readers can refer to Ellis's essay to read another, perhaps more extensive, examination of the phenomenon of African American bynames.

3. Students' opinions about Gates's parents' own use of prejudicial words may vary. Before addressing this question, students may find it helpful to review Gloria Naylor's essay, "The Meanings of a Word," in Chapter 4 and in particular her discussion of words set within unique contexts and inflections, as well as her examination of her extended family's use of the term *nigger*.

4. The striking thing about the way Mr. Wilson is described in paragraph 4 is that despite Wilson's generally silent and unfriendly demeanor, Gates's father had managed to break through the brooding exterior to establish a kind of familiarity with him, enough so that they always spoke to each other. This bond of familiarity makes Gates's discovery that Mr. Wilson calls his father "George" all the more confusing and all the more painful.

Classroom Activity Using Narration

When discussing the results of this exercise, be sure that you examine the ways in which students deal with lapses in chronological order so that they avoid causing confusion for readers. Pay particular attention to the kinds of connections they make between paragraphs that show significant breaks in the chronological arrangement of events. After looking at students' strategies for narrating events out of sequence, discuss the variety of ways writers can achieve continuity and coherence when disrupting the chronology of their narration.

White Lies (p. 381)
■ **Erin Murphy**

Essay Analysis and Discussion

In the concluding paragraph, Murphy says that she does not remember her role and cannot even say for sure whether she saw Connie with her mother in the store. With so much ambiguity, why then would Murphy name her essay "White Lies"? Do students think that Murphy herself lied? If Connie did lie about her father's job at the factory, would that have been a "white lie"? Discuss with the class the difference between so-called white lies and regular lies. Who determines which is which? Ask students if they can think of other names for the kind of lie Connie might have told. A protective lie or a lie for social acceptance might be more descriptive.

Thinking Critically about This Reading

In this story, Murphy uses the idea of "perhapsing" to show that sometimes your memories are not reliable, and in this case, the unreliability was probably a factor of shame or regret. In her quote, Murphy says that this type of remembering establishes her as a reliable narrator, simply because it is not realistic to remember every detail about an event that happened in fifth grade. Most readers will be able to relate to looking back on something and wishing that they had done something differently. Murphy takes that inclination one step further to say that she does not exactly remember what happened but, perhaps, that is because she does not want to.

Questions for Study and Discussion

1. Student responses may vary, although many may be impressed with Murphy's ability to move so quickly, clearly, and steadily through the narrative without losing the reader. Her details—like the specific names Connie was called or the type of candy the narrator may have asked for—bring the story to life.

2. Murphy reiterates her teacher's lesson that certain adjectives like *special* and *different* have no superlatives. There is no "perfectest" or "differentest," but in reality, Murphy notes, one can be more different than another. In her example, Connie was the most different in the class, giving Arpi some breathing room.

3. Student answers may vary. Murphy seems to have been an observer and probable participant in requesting candy from Connie, if not a part of the group who mocked her. The narrator obviously feels guilty for her role in the situation, but is uncertain exactly what that role was.

4. Murphy saw the classroom teacher as apathetic, unobservant and nonreactive. She includes the information about the teacher probably because most readers will wonder why the teacher did not do anything to protect Connie. The laissez-faire teacher also demonstrates Connie's early lesson that adults cannot always be trusted to protect the innocent.

5. Student answers may vary. One point of Connie's story is that what adults teach and the reality of the world are often *different*. She reminds readers that children's worlds are often painful and complicated, too. The teacher's

grammatical rules and her disinterest in engaging with the class left the children to manage themselves. Children are vulnerable, but they can be terribly cruel; being different is difficult and, without the protection of an adult, often unbearable. Only Connie's mother, if she really did take her daughter to the 7-Eleven to buy candy, was engaged in the child's world.

6. Student answers will vary. Some will empathize with Connie's mother, who did what she could to change her daughter's social status at school. Others may think that she was teaching her daughter to buy acceptance instead of standing up for herself. Perhaps the mother understood that Connie's social status would not change without drastic efforts, and she was doing what she could to protect her daughter.

7. Connie's mother most likely wants to protect her child socially. Seeing her daughter in pain, she tried to help Connie be treated better in school. Student answers regarding what they might have done may vary. Some might say that they would have talked to the teacher or taught Connie how to stick up for herself.

Classroom Activity Using Narration

During this activity, you might also want to ask students how leaving out information can be perceived as a "white lie." Perhapsing is a way of acknowledging that some information might be missing. To not mislead an audience, acknowledging gaps in information is as important as what fills the other gaps. In an investigation, for example, a witness may have to account for every activity in which he or she engaged that evening. If the witness leaves out, for example, dropping off the neighbor's kids, that omission can be equated to a lie. Acknowledging gaps with perhapsing or other strategies maintains the author and essay's integrity.

Momma, the Dentist, and Me (p. 386)
■ Maya Angelou

Essay Analysis and Discussion

The editors of this text placed their own title on this selection from Angelou's *I Know Why the Caged Bird Sings*. Their title is appropriate for the content of the essay, but given the complexity of Angelou's narration, other suitable options may also exist. This essay can therefore serve as a catalyst for a discussion of how to choose an effective title. Ask your students to reread the essay with an eye toward providing it with a new title. Then, have them write suggested titles on slips of paper and turn them in so that you can compile an anonymous listing on the board. Once you have completed the list, ask the students to vote on which title they like best, and when they have indicated their preferences, discuss why some titles were chosen over others. You will want to consider originality, ability to stimulate interest, and appropriateness to the content of the essay, as well as other factors the students may see as significant.

Thinking Critically about This Reading

Angelou goes on to say that on the white side of town, "[i]f the pain didn't diminish then, the familiar yet strange sights hypnotized me into believing that it had" (paragraph 6). Angelou's tooth began to hurt again when she passed the jail and encountered white children who taunted her. Angelou's pain relief is a metaphor for the contrasts between the black side of town (raw, painful) and the white side of town (protected, soothing).

Questions for Study and Discussion

1. Angelou's purpose is to show the kind of pain that bigotry and injustice inflict and to show that such cruelty often fosters the desire for retribution in its victims.

2. The content of the two interchanges between Momma and the dentist is similar in that, in both cases, Momma exacts revenge on the dentist for his refusal to treat the young girl. But the way she achieves that revenge is different. In Maya's version, Momma "obliterates" the dentist with her angry words, rendering him weak and submissive under her power and authority. In Momma's version, although she speaks of the dentist and his nurse with contempt, the scene she describes is more subdued and less vengeful, but ultimately more productive in getting Maya's toothache treated. The style of the two versions is notably different. To use Angelou's words, the first displays an "eloquent command of English," both in the way Momma speaks and in Maya's description of events, while in the second, Momma uses her usual vernacular to recall the scene.

3. Angelou's chronological presentation helps her establish a clear and purposeful context for the scene at the dentist's office. In the narration leading up to the visit, she builds a sense of tension and frustration as she describes the pain of her toothache and her anxiety about approaching a white dentist. The chronological pattern also helps juxtapose the two versions of what occurred between Momma and the dentist. The first-person point of view is crucial to the central idea of the essay because it shows Maya's desire for retribution firsthand, a desire that creates the fantasized version of the confrontation between Momma and the dentist. Her version becomes more poignant because readers come to feel what she is like and what motivates her before they reach that scene. This empathy or understanding that builds up on the part of the reader makes the final statement more potent.

4. Angelou's essay contains the following similes: "as if a whitebreeze blew off the whitefolks and cushioned everything in their neighborhood" (6);

76

"the way people hunt for shells" (18); "like little claps of thunder" (29); "like filling in a pie crust" (46); "like a piece of lint" (48); "thick as thieves" (48); and "like he was sitting on a pin" (48). Each simile works within its paragraph, and all the similes work together to provide a more vivid description of events.

5. Angelou's version of the episode describes what, for her, is a more just resolution of the situation: a Dodge City–style triumph over bigotry. The dentist is not only confronted, he is driven from town frightened and disgraced. To the child, it must have been a small consolation that the dentist had to pay a few more dollars on his debt to the grandmother.

6. Angelou first uses exaggerated descriptions to indicate the magnitude of her pain: "I prayed earnestly that I'd be allowed to sit under the house and have the building collapse on my left jaw" (1); "seriously considering the idea of jumping in the well" (2); "I was certain that I'd be dead" (2); "the pain was more serious than that which anyone had ever suffered" (3). She then presents some startling metaphors to show her intimate connection to that pain: "I had frozen to the pain" (4); "the pain was my world, an aura that haloed me for three feet around" (5). These references are important because they establish the extent to which she suffers physically, yet the physical pain subsides when Maya confronts the psychic pain of bigotry and injustice described in paragraphs 9 through 26, culminating in the dentist's refusal to treat her.

Classroom Activity Using Narration

Making a list rather than drafting is the important part of this activity. It's far easier for students to see a sequence of activities, and how it may be reordered, in list form than in a paragraph or essay. It is useful to discuss how drama is achieved through placement at the beginning or end of a sequence and what it takes to create rising tension in a sequence of events.

The Story of an Hour (p. 395)
■ **Kate Chopin**

Essay Analysis and Discussion

Chopin lived in an era when women had few options. Those who did not marry and manage their family's household were referred to in pejorative terms such as "old maid" and "spinster" if they were known to be chaste, and as "eccentric" or worse if they had the hint of scandal about them. "The Story of an Hour" would not have much effect in these days of no-fault divorce and ever-increasing career opportunities for women, but taken in the context of its time, it is a compelling story that raises many issues of the day. The prereading prompt asks students to consider marriage on personal terms. Before students read the story, it may be a good idea to discuss what marriage meant for both men and women in the early 1900s. Some students may know something about married life in that era, but they probably have not thought about it much as a reality. What is it like to be bound to someone with no hope of ever being released if the relationship sours? The swift progression of Mrs. Mallard's emotions—and she was married to a gentle man whom she was able to love at least some of the time—communicates how stifling the situation could be in Chopin's eyes.

Thinking Critically about This Reading

Her feeling of freedom is improper. One is not supposed to feel great joy so soon after the death of a spouse, so the natural reaction would be to fight it, at least initially.

Questions for Study and Discussion

1. Mrs. Mallard's friends and relatives see nothing other than pure grief at first, and they assume that she remains in that state. Her actual feelings are much more complicated. They include grief but are mixed with large portions of relief and joy.

2. Chopin is setting the scene in which Mrs. Mallard's epiphany is to occur. The descriptions distance the reader from the strong emotional nature of the situation. They establish that life is going on around her, even though she is in a state of suspended thought. The section effectively bridges the gap between the abrupt beginning of the story and the dominant reaction Mrs. Mallard has to her husband's supposed death, and it allows Chopin to acquaint the reader with Mrs. Mallard's physical setting.

3. The swift progression of Mrs. Mallard's emotions communicates the stifling effect marriage had on women. A more gradual, thought-out reaction would not have the same effect, because once the grief has passed, the pleasure of regaining personal freedom is not a startling thing for the widow to feel. For her to feel it within an hour is startling, and by using the time element in her title, Chopin ensures that the reader does not miss the point.

4. The fictional narrative allows her to place thoughts in Mrs. Mallard's head, and it allows her to manipulate the events of the story to present her point. The psychology of marriage is something that would have been difficult for her to write about on a factual basis—especially in such a patriarchal society—but fiction is a medium in which she can present her point of view clearly and dramatically.

5. On an obvious level, Chopin couldn't have Mrs. Mallard narrate her own story because she is dead at the end. Chopin uses a third-person narrator so that we can observe Mrs. Mallard's reactions to the news of her husband's apparent death and her subsequent realization that she was now "free, free,

free!" The third-person narrator's description of Louise Mallard as "a goddess of Victory" sets readers up for Brently Mallard's surprise appearance and for the final irony in Chopin's concluding sentence.

Classroom Activity Using Narration

The sentence progression is 3, 5, 2, 1, 4. Students may need to revise their first try at writing their own paragraph, because the exercise demands that the sentences be linked strongly to one another before they are scrambled. Writing about a progression of events without falling into a plodding, monotonous style of writing can be difficult, but students should try to make their paragraphs as interesting and smoothly linked as possible.

CHAPTER 15 **Description**

The Corner Store (p. 402)
■ **Eudora Welty**

Essay Analysis and Discussion

Welty makes good use of detail and organization as she moves through the corner store of her childhood. In a few words, she manages to fill our minds as full as Mr. Sessions fills his shelves. Notice how Welty uses sensory description to paint a picture that is real, without overusing detail. Also, students can analyze the way Welty acquaints us with Mr. Sessions without having him speak. Then students can discuss the author's use of hard detail as contrasted with her poetic impressions. The exercise will help them understand how difficult it is to say enough without saying too much.

Thinking Critically about This Reading

Mr. Sessions brings life and personality to the collection of things Welty sees and describes. He is the friendly man behind the counter who remembers each customer's weight and favorite flavor of soda. The store gives the community a common gathering place and a point of common reference.

Questions for Study and Discussion

1. Students will find examples of chronological and spatial organization throughout the essay. Welty organizes the essay chronologically through the sequence of events from the time she enters the store until she leaves. Her body movement around the store and the movement of her eyes as she looks over the shelves and the counters are examples of spatial organization.

2. Welty realizes that a person who comes into a store out of the bright sun-light initially feels almost blind. Therefore, the first things that a person would be aware of are the odors—in this case, of licorice, dill pickle brine, ammonia, and untrapped mice.

3. Welty creates an impression of the old-fashioned plenty associated with a twentieth-century country store by describing shelves, counters, and barrels stocked with the numberless goodies and smells available in such places.

4. Mr. Sessions is warm and friendly, a man who invites a child's hand to reach for a choice of penny candies, who knows what the child's favorite drink is, who weighs small children on his scale before they leave the store, and who will "remember what you weighed the last time."

5. Welty puts certain phrases in parentheses to set them apart. This informa-tion characterizes the era in even more detail than the rest of the essay. A personal quality, which identifies the things that were especially dear to the writer, would be lost if these asides to the reader were left out.

6. Students should give reasons that demonstrate their understanding of end-ings.

Classroom Activity Using Description

It ought to be fun to see the variety of alternative terms the students are capable of producing. You may want to see if students all have the same dominant im-pression of the classroom and see if that impression depends on what is focused on. For example, if one student focuses on the people, he might have the im-pression of the classroom as being a positive place filled with friends. Another student focusing on the lack of windows and the buzzing sound of the lights might give the room the impression of a cage.

And the Orchestra Played On (p. 407)
■ Joanne Lipman

Essay Analysis and Discussion

This essay first appeared in the *New York Times*. Ask students why they think a newspaper such as the *Times* would be interested in such a story. Why might this story be an appropriate one for a New York–based publication? Mr. K. was a Ukrainian immigrant, and his story appeals to the immigrant history of New York and the experience interacting with them and their "foreign" ways. Ask students how Lipman highlights his differences without mocking him. Pointing out someone's quirks can sometimes be insulting. Discuss how Lip-man's ability to demonstrate respect allows her to discuss the more quirky parts of Mr. K.'s personality.

In this essay, the author also remembers fondly someone who has now died. This essay can be discussed in conjunction with Tobias Wolff's "The Last Shot," in which he fondly remembers a fellow service man, Hugh. Discuss these essays together and how they pay tribute to those who have died by highlighting simple yet telling aspects of their personality.

Thinking Critically about This Reading

In paragraph 4, Lipman talks about how hard Mr. K. pushed the students. In this paragraph, she tells the reader that she and the other students loved him, even if they did not know it at the time. She tells us that her love for him caused her to "frantically" search for her instrument to play at his funeral. A great teacher inspires students into action. Those around Mr. K. also seemed to continue playing beyond their time with him. His daughter and others went on to play professionally. He must have given them the foundation on which to build. Despite his harsh methods, many continued with their instruments, causing a lifelong love of music. Given how much the students enjoyed playing together, he seemed to be able to teach people how to connect through music. Most students will be convinced that he is a teacher to be remembered, if as much for his harshness and curious commentary as for his ability to instill the love of music and teach the fundamentals.

Questions for Study and Discussion

1. Student answers will vary. Many will say that Mr. K. sounds strict, tough, or intense because he "berated" the students for the sound of their instruments, their posture, and their counting. He also made them endure long practice sessions. Lipman says that he pushed them harder than their parents did. Some students may say that he seemed like an angry and controlling perfectionist. Her recounting of his past would help some understand that in a life dominated and controlled by so many outside forces (sickness, Nazis, murder), a man like Mr. K. might have looked to music as the one thing he could control.

2. Mr. K.'s amusing use of similes when berating students softens his image. Had Lipman not quoted him, he might have sounded simply angry and tough. These quotes give him personality. They are especially amusing given that they come from a man for whom English is a second language. The quotes allow Mr. K. to represent himself, rather than making him simply an image of Lipman's memory and telling.

3. By making paragraph 5 one sentence, Lipman highlights the irony of Mr. K.'s brutal rehearsals. His ability to instill fear, his high standards, and his relentlessness made students love him, not despise him. Had she included this sentence at the end of the paragraph, the point could have been lost or

simply made no sense. The sentence prior—"He scared the daylights out of us" (4)—would have also lost power had it been quickly followed. She needed to build up his image as a fear-evoking character, before descending back into love. Paragraphs helped create that tension and release.

4. To substantiate her story and add color, Lipman talks about the careers of and distances traveled by other students. Otherwise, this essay could have become one about her love for her teacher instead of a story about the teacher. Also, the details validate her earlier comment that "we loved him." The careers and distances traveled showed that, indeed, many loved him.

5. The enduring lesson was the power of music to bond people.

6. The point of the story is the power of music to inspire and move people for a lifetime: Music is a gift. For the little girl, the music played at her brother's funeral (organized by Mr. K.) stayed with her for her whole life. It was so powerful that she hopped on a plane to say "thank you" and chose to become a professional musician.

7. Student opinions about the ending will differ. Some may find it powerful. You may want to ask students to consider how the essay would have read had Lipman left out the last line. Is the last line necessary? With the last sentence, the essay ties into first paragraph, about why she was rummaging through her closet. She was doing so to find her viola, her instrument with which *she* would say, "Thank you."

Classroom Activity Using Description

Remind students that when using metaphors and similes, freshness and consistency are important factors. To describe someone who is fidgeting in a way that is both clichéd and inconsistent, one could say the person is "as nervous as a cat with ants in his pants" or is "bouncing off the walls like a bull in a china shop." A more fresh and consistent description of a fidgeter might say, "The nervous host set and reset the table as though it were a Rubik's Cube with no solution."

To complete this activity, you might want to have your students envision different scenarios and write brief descriptions that are almost like one-sentence short stories. For example, to express the idea of finger-lacing, a student might write, "As the interviewer approached, the job applicant unwove the damp mat of her hands and dried them on the waiting-room chair." To describe someone breathing rapidly, a student could write, "I have always been afraid of roller-coasters because they make my adrenalin surge and my breathing become the shallow panting of a doomed fish." To describe someone who is squirming or tapping an object, a student could write, "Throughout the long test, the person next to me sat with his left leg crossed over his right, rhythmically beating his airborne foot up and down at the ankle, as though marking time with a metronome."

Yarn (p. 412)

■ **Kyoko Mori**

Essay Analysis and Discussion

Mori's audience is presumably not just people who like to knit. She focuses on the shared human experience of disliking something initially, but then reclaiming it later. Do students have hobbies that they have dropped or some activity that turned them off as a child that they reclaimed later in life? A description of Mori's process of dropping and reclaiming a hobby is something to which many can relate. Her description, although about knitting specifically, focuses enough on her personal experience that a wider audience can relate. This essay can be a reminder that even though everyone might not be interested in the same sport, topic, or hobby, a powerful written description can compel even skeptical readers.

Thinking Critically about This Reading

Because Mori created many mittens to complete the assignment successfully, the readers know that she is someone who does not give up easily. This early failure is what made her more determined to succeed later. Knitting represented a challenge she would take on for the rest of her life.

Questions for Study and Discussion

1. Mittens are the worst project for beginners because they are so difficult to complete correctly. Specifically, mitten knitting must occur in a tub, with four needles that slip and twist easily; any extra stitch, lack of stitch, or incorrect tightness throws off the perfect precision needed to make mittens correctly. Mori says that knitters can easily accidentally make two of the same hand. Sweaters are easier because they do not require patterns, they are more forgiving if the stitches are not perfect in number or tightness, and errors are not visible when the sweater is worn.

2. Sabrina helped Mori release her earlier experience by helping her connect with the love of knitting and separating that from the perfectionism required to make mittens. The sweater knitting Sabrina introduced to Mori was a relaxed way for Mori to start again. No patterns were required, and small errors did not destroy the whole project. The quotes from Sabrina demonstrate how she helped free Mori from her earlier experience. By quoting Sabrina directly, Mori *shows* instead of *tells* Sabrina's philosophy on knitting.

3. Inside each yarn store, Mori says, "the walls are lined with plastic crates bursting with color" (paragraph 10). In addition to color, she describes the variety of yarn—rayon chenille, angoras, alpacas, silk blends, and cotton blends. Students will have different impressions of a yarn store, but most will say it sounds colorful, soft, cozy, or warm.

4. Mori uses two similes in paragraph 12 to highlight the contrast between the finished and the unfinished hat. Mori describes her unfinished mohair hat as looking "more like a lamp shade." Then, with some washing this hat transforms finally, looking "like a professionally made bowler." In paragraph 13, she describes the antique mall as feeling "like three city blocks crammed with furniture and knick-knacks." This description helps the reader get a sense of the size and density of the mall.

5. Yarn is forgiving in that for certain projects, sweaters and scarves, knitters can make mistakes and easily adjust midproject. Unlike mittens, you can still have an acceptable finished product even in the absence of perfect knitting.

6. She most likely liked the hat because of the dramatic transformation that takes place when it is put into the washing machine and because of the professional-looking end product. She graduates on to different products because after some time the hat no longer challenged her, and challenge is what she sought. In paragraph 14, she says, "I would rather knit from a complicated pattern and make a few mistakes than execute an easier one flawlessly."

7. In the end, by rejecting the yellow yarn that represented her failure and frustration with knitting, she reclaims the craft. In the beginning, she discusses how she disliked the color yellow as much as she disliked failing at the mittens. Through the various phases described in her essay, however, she was able to release the yellow and reclaim her "hunger for color" (10).

Classroom Activity Using Description

An example for "thoughtful" could be the following:

- Remembers birthdays
- Asks about sick family members
- Makes soup for friends when sick
- Bought father tickets for himself and his friends to a sports team he loves

Encourage students to then do several others together as a class. The exercise will push them and is worth continuing beyond one example.

The Taj Mahal (p. 419)
■ Salman Rushdie

Essay Analysis and Discussion

Stress in the discussion how the overdescription of something can distract people from the thing itself. Ask students for examples. One interesting example is a new word introduced in 1968 called "compassion fatigue." This word was introduced in the United States to describe how people have become burnt out on charitable contributions because they have received too many requests for too many important causes. In a way, how might this compassion fatigue be similar to Rushdie's description? He talks about how important it is to *see* something in person; otherwise, the clichéd images will take over. How would it be different to see a village destroyed by a flood versus simply receiving a photo of it with a contribution request? Ask students to find some other places, situations, or images that have become so overused that they have lost their effect.

Thinking Critically about This Reading

It is difficult for a writer to make people "see" a place or thing through the writer's eyes if the reader has already seen multiple images. Early explorers and writers had the advantage when explaining faraway places to people who had never left their villages and had an easier time inserting themselves into the reader's mind. Students will believe that Rushdie succeeded to various degrees. He convinces the reader that one must see the Taj Mahal in person, but because he does not describe the building in great detail, he did not help people "see it." He wanted to convince them to go see it.

Questions for Study and Discussion

1. Repeated images take away the unique charm.
2. "Every hustler and hawker in Agra" (paragraph 3) awaits visitors at the outer walls of the gardens. Seeing something too much can lead to hatred for it. See the Essay Analysis and Discussion description of compassion fatigue above.
3. Rushdie had been skeptical about his first visit, but he says that the building "left his skepticism in shreds" (5). He said that the counterfeit images were destroyed when he saw the real thing. He italicized "thing-in-itself" to emphasize the difference between the truth and imitation (3). He believes that people must see the building because "the sound is truer than the echo" (6). He knows that no matter what he writes about the Taj Mahal, it will never be as powerful as seeing it himself.
4. The cruel tales are a stark contrast to the beauty.
5. He uses contrast in his transitions. He discusses his skepticism in one paragraph and then switches to the reality of the beauty in the next, such as between paragraphs 4 and 5. Again at the end of paragraph 5, he contrasts the effect of the counterfeits on the psyche to paragraph 6 when he brings us back to the real.
6. Because the physical details have been so often described, he focuses on the effect that the building had on him and in doing so hopes to encourage

others to visit in person. He knows that readers will just ignore repeating the stereotypical images.

Classroom Activity Using Description

> *go:* move, fling, run, drive, find, get-up-and-go, zest
> *see:* catch a glimpse of, behold, gape, gaze, inspect
> *say:* announce, declare, convey, divulge, affirm
> *throw:* bombard, fling, flick, fire, pitch, shove, catapult
> *take:* abduct, abstract, carry off, confiscate, nab, snatch
> *drink:* consume, down, gulp, slurp, swig
> *exercise:* cultivate, improve, hone, pump iron, rehearse, work out
> *study:* apply oneself, bone up, brood over, burn midnight oil, mull over, read up, hit the books
> *sleep:* bed down, hit the sack, nod off, sack out, slumber, snooze, repose

CHAPTER 16 **Process Analysis**

The Principles of Poor Writing (p. 427)
■ **Paul W. Merrill**

Essay Analysis and Discussion

In this process analysis piece, the author seemingly teaches his readers how to write poorly. In fact, he is using irony to teach good writing skills. He wants readers to do as he does, not as he says. Readers know immediately that Merrill does not follow his own advice, because he gives his readers an essay that engages his audience, uses simple and clear examples, and clearly went through the process of revision. While reading his ironic instructions, many students will wonder which of these writing mistakes they make. Keeping one's readers in mind at all times might be a new concept for students. Unlike writing a birthday card, which surely keeps the reader in mind, much academic writing or personal writing can quickly lose touch with the world beyond the writer. Revision is the process most people tend to avoid, because they are pleased just to have completed their papers on time. Usually not enough time is planned for revising. Instances of verbosity may be harder for students to identify in their own writing. Maybe students copy the writing styles of other vague academics because they think that is the acceptable academic style. Some professors may reward this behavior if they write in a similar style.

Thinking Critically about This Reading

In his career, Merrill has undoubtedly read thousands of scientific articles and written hundreds of his own. He has seen multiple examples of good writing and, most likely, even more examples of bad. The stereotype is that scientists are notorious for their inability to communicate well through writing, having been trained in science rather than English or the humanities. Merrill believes that scientists must write well so as to communicate their findings and expand human knowledge. If no one can understand them, what good is all that research? Astronomy is already complicated enough without adding verbose language and leaving readers to fend for themselves. Merrill suggests that scientists and all writers need to take more responsibility for the quality of their writing. They must engage their reader and treat him or her like a friend.

Questions for Study and Discussion

1. Most students will suspect from the title that this essay is ironic, and the introduction and actual advice will confirm that. Because the title is so absurd, the reader can assume that Merrill wants people to know that the essay will be ironic.

2. Merrill's essay is directional. He provides, albeit ironically, a step-by-step guide on "how to write poorly." Rather than a general informational process piece on bad writing, he provides a recipe for bad writing: (1) Ignore the reader; (2) be verbose, vague, and pompous; and (3) do not revise.

3. Although Merrill writes an ironic piece on bad writing, he actually wants his readers to learn the skills for good writing. To do so, he has provided a well-crafted essay in which even the order of his directives is instructional. First, when beginning an essay, the writer needs to identify the audience. For example, is the audience educated on the topic, or is it a general audience? Second, in the actual content of the essay, the writer must establish a writing style that helps rather than impedes the readers' ability to understand. Using vague or verbose language will lose the audience. Finally, writers must revise to ensure that the essay holds together, is written in complete sentences, and has some sort of natural flow.

4. Most students will appreciate the examples provided. If they cannot see some of their own mistakes, surely they have seen similar examples in their reading. Students may not agree with all the examples. For instance, perhaps they prefer razzle-dazzle language over simple and direct statements.

5. The ironic title catches the readers' attention and provides a new spin on an old topic. Hundreds of people have written books and essays on good writing. Students have probably been told many times about their mistakes, yet poor writing can still be found everywhere. Perhaps people have been tuning out the more straightforward writing lessons. With irony, Merrill might be able to get people to catch themselves in the act of sloppy

writing and then self-correct. The disadvantage could be that readers too easily dismiss his idea or, less likely, miss the irony. When an essay is ironic, it sometimes has a lighter tone, causing some readers to possibly distance themselves from the message being presented.

6. When presenting a subject that has been written about many times, irony can engage readers. Irony also helps writers highlight bad behavior and can show readers this behavior in themselves, without the writer having to accuse them directly.

Classroom Activity Using Process Analysis

Preface this activity by telling your students that they need to avoid assuming knowledge on the part of the reader. Students are usually surprised at how difficult it is to write a process analysis so that a true novice can follow the steps. Even directing a simple task, like scrambling eggs, is a challenge when the directions are for someone who has never been in a kitchen. The student reviews should be stringent—"beat the eggs" could lead to disastrous results if not properly explained in the paper.

How to Make Chocolate Sauce (p. 433)
■ Nicholson Baker

Essay Analysis and Discussion

Baker's essay delights because he takes something we have seen many times—a recipe—and plays with it. He makes instructions warm, personal, and intimate. Ask students how the same might be done with an instruction manual. Would that be possible, or are some instructions just too dry to make fun? What details could a writer add that could describe in the same tone fixing a bike chain? For example, the feel of the bike grease on your fingers, the weight of the chain, and the sound of the pedals rotating would all contribute to the more sensory, rather than intellectual, understanding of what it means to fix a chain. Writers can engage different senses.

Thinking Critically about This Reading

Unlike most recipes, Baker's does not begin with a list of ingredients, servings created, and the amounts of each and time required followed by a numbered list of steps. Instead, it reads like a narrative. By presenting the recipe as he did, Baker shared with the reader not only the "how" of the chocolate sauce, but the "why." He invites the reader into the sensual experience of making the sauce. One downside might be that readers might find it difficult to actually follow the recipe, so it is not entirely practical.

Questions for Study and Discussion

1. For the most part, Baker's narrative is clear. He is clear about ingredients and quantity. He leaves out some important information such as the recommended temperature to melt the chocolate, the total time required to complete the process, and the servings generated. He could add these pieces of information for greater clarity.

2. Most students will say that his process is easy to follow. This method might be difficult for pastries or meats that require specific temperature and time requirements. Sauces and soups are perfect for this style.

3. Baker's style is suited to recipes because he brings the reader with him at every step. Details help him describe the process in a reader-friendly way. He even gives the recipe follower something to do while the chocolate is melting. Readers almost have the sense that he is holding their hand through the process, which is the feeling one seeks when looking to a recipe. Details show his sensitivity to the reader's experience. It shows a presence.

4. Examples of descriptive language are *subsiding chunk of butter, drifts of confectioners' sugar, paste-like, tappable chocolate,* and *complete trellis-work.* The descriptive language helps readers understand not just the mechanics, but also the sensory indicators that will guide them through the process.

5. *Velouté* is a French word; it could be considered a technical cooking word as it means a soup enriched with fresh cream and egg. Baker uses the word here in its more colloquial French usage, meaning a heavy, soup-like consistency. *Fragonard,* also French, refers to a company that produces a variety of perfumes. Here Baker used rather sophisticated word play (or as the French say, "jeux de mots") because in French, ice-cream flavors are called "parfums de glace," or "perfumes of ice cream"' thus these terms explain why he uses a French perfume company to describe flavors of ice cream. *Fragonard* is not a technical cooking word.

6. Some students might describe his tone as *sensual, sweet,* or *generous.* His recipe goes beyond simple mechanical instructions and inspires the reader to connect with the sensuality of the creation. Chocolate sauce is a rich, sensual delicacy, and Baker writes his description in a way that honors the spirit of the task as well as the task itself.

Classroom Activity Using Process Analysis

Students have fun with this activity. It's an exercise in following written directions. Even though each student is following the same set of directions, don't be surprised if their astro tubes don't look alike. Ask students whether any of the directions were difficult to follow, and, if so, how those directions might be improved. Ask students whether they relied primarily on the written or the visual directions. Finally, recalling the specific directions in steps 6 and 9, have students fly their tubes.

Why Leaves Turn Color in the Fall (p. 438)
■ Diane Ackerman

Essay Analysis and Discussion

Try comparing the process description in Ackerman's essay with that of Nicholson Baker in "How to Make Chocolate Sauce." Although giving directions is different than explaining a scientific process, they are both detailed step-by-step descriptions. You may want to ask students to take a few minutes in class to write about the changing of the leaves in Baker's style so that they can feel the difference. They would need to remove the scientific language or perhaps even write it from the tree's perspective. Stylistically, Ackerman's essay explains but is not poetic or romantic as Baker's essay. One is more poetic, but they both explain.

Thinking Critically about This Reading

By attributing human qualities to nature and trees, Ackerman draws a parallel between the life cycle of leaves and of humans. She is asking the reader to think of the season cycle as similar to the human life cycle.

Questions for Study and Discussion

1. A reduction in sunlight, which occurs as the days grow shorter in the fall, causes leaves to change color (paragraph 2). The brightest colors of autumn are in the United States and in eastern China, where a rich climate exists. The cold nights and sunny days give the maples their deep red in the United States. She says that the strongest colors occur when the fall sunlight is strong and the nights are cool and dry.
2. During summer, the tree withdraws nutrients from its leaves back into its trunk and roots. The leaves lose nourishment and no longer produce chlorophyll. The loss of the chlorophyll removes the green and reveals the underlying bright colors that were always there (paragraph 2).
3. Student opinions will vary. Most will probably find her descriptions quite clear and the process analysis useful. The more detail she offers, the more the reader can appreciate the beauty and complexity of the process. Detail leads to appreciation.
4. Ackerman's organization is chronological, mirroring and reinforcing the process she explains. She begins by describing how the leaves' color changes at the beginning of fall "catches one unaware" (1) and ends with fallen leaves' accumulation on the ground as the winter approaches. Each of her explanations begins with how people observe and interact with the natural

world and ends with the science behind the observable phenomena. This organization enables a general audience to connect their own experiences with fall to Ackerman's scientific explanation of the underlying processes of the season.

5. Similes and metaphors are figures of speech that make writing vivid and interesting. Ackerman's similes and metaphors draw upon the natural and serve to further engage her readers with her subject. Examples of her similes include "keen-eyed as leopards" (1); "rattle like tiny gourds" (1), "flashes like a marquee" (4); "piles of leaves ... like confetti" (8), and "stuccolike mortar" (10). Examples of her metaphors include "sunlight rules most living things with its golden edicts" (2) and "they glide and swoop, rocking in invisible cradles" (9).

6. Ackerman's concluding sentence reinforces the idea of the ever-turning nature of life—the continual birth, development, and death that occur in the natural world. It makes sense to end with this sentiment at the *end* of the essay. All things come to an end, even the essay.

Classroom Activity Using Process Analysis

A most wonderful exercise in class is the following. This exercise has been done repeatedly in college classes and makes the point so well. Hand out index cards, and ask each student to write out exactly how to make a peanut butter and jelly sandwich. At the front of the room, the teacher has sliced bread in a bag, a new jar of peanut butter, a new jar of jelly, and a butter knife. Collect the index cards, choose one, and follow it exactly. The students will never tell you *how* to open the bag of bread. When the card starts with, say, "Take two slices of bread," pick up the bag of bread and look at how to open it as if you have never seen one before. Just rip the plastic from the center and watch the bread fall everywhere. Then when the instruction is "Spread peanut butter," pick up the knife and peanut butter quizzically wondering how to open it. Slam the knife through the lid. Students will get the point quickly. When explaining something, it is always dangerous to assume anything.

CHAPTER 17 **Definition**

What Is Crime? (p. 447)
■ **Lawrence M. Friedman**

Essay Analysis and Discussion

Friedman offers readers a discussion of crime from a legal perspective. Many readers are surprised by what does not constitute a crime. On the other hand,

Friedman points out that society decides what is a crime. This essay lends itself to some interesting writing activities. Have students pick two or three of Friedman's examples of noncrimes, such as breaking a contract, cheating on a spouse, poor driving, and overcharging at restaurants. Have them argue both for and against making these actual crimes, according to the legal definition. What would be gained or lost by making these crimes? Remind them of the different legal ramifications, according to the essay. You may also have them debate other issues, like the decriminalization of marijuana.

Thinking Critically about This Reading

Friedman states that society deems illegal that which upsets the stability of society. First comes the social judgment, then comes the legal judgment.

Questions for Study and Discussion

1. According to Friedman, crime "is a *legal* concept" (paragraph 1); what makes some conduct criminal and other conduct not is that some acts, but not others, are "against the law" (1).
2. In a criminal case, "society is the victim, along with the 'real' victim" (3). The crime can be punished without the victim's consent, and the state pays for the prosecution. In civil cases, the defendant cannot be incarcerated and does not receive a criminal record. The injured party manages and pays for the case, not the state. The case can be dropped.
3. Society is the victim because it has decided that the criminal act harms everyone, not just the individual. Student answers to the second part of the question will vary.
4. He cites lying, cheating on a spouse, overcharging on restaurant bills, and psychological abuse as examples of awful acts that are not considered crimes. He also cites breaking contracts, driving carelessly, slandering, and infringing copyrights as examples of acts that, while detrimental to society, are not considered crimes.
5. Friedman wants readers to remember that the legal status of a behavior does not necessarily determine the negative effect it has on the culture. Although breaking contracts or cheating on spouses can have a hugely detrimental effect on those involved, it is society that determines which acts are crimes. He wants readers to see the role they play in determining which acts are legally considered a crime rather than a civil offense.

Classroom Activity Using Definition

This simple exercise in critical thinking requires that students see a given item as being both a part of some larger class of items that share certain characteristics as well as differentiated from the other members of that class by certain distinguishing features. Not all students will be able to differentiate a tenor saxophone from other types of saxophones in the woodwind instrument class, so it may be necessary to have someone in the class who knows this narrower subject area offer assistance. (You may want to prepare yourself for the possibility that no one knows that the saxophone is a nineteenth-century invention of Adolphe Sax and that there are eight types of saxophone, each representing a different tonal range. Of these eight types, only four are widely used: the B-flat soprano, the E-flat alto, the B-flat tenor, and the E-flat baritone.)

The Company Man (p. 451)
■ **Ellen Goodman**

Essay Analysis and Discussion

Ellen Goodman's essay, like W. H. Auden's poem "The Unknown Citizen," uses irony and sarcasm to expose Americans' penchant for becoming workaholics. Goodman develops her definition of "company man" by carefully showing readers what Phil is as well as what he is not. Ask students if they make a distinction between a *company man* and a *workaholic*. Have them share their own experiences with a parent, relative, or friend who is a "company man" or workaholic and describe the defining personality traits of that person. Explore the reasons why some people become overinvolved with their schooling or careers to the exclusion of other facets of their lives (for example, recreation, relationships, or health). Finally, ask students what they think will be their own priorities after they graduate and take a job.

Thinking Critically about This Reading

This statement illustrates how small a presence Phil had in his own home and with his own family. Phil and his youngest son were essentially familiar strangers whose only commonality was that they shared a roof, much like neighbors in an apartment building who know each other by sight but speak no more than the occasional hello as they come and go.

Questions for Study and Discussion

1. Although some people look at a company man in a positive light—an employee who is reliable and shows extreme loyalty to his employer—Goodman does not. She calls Phil—the company man in this case—a "workaholic" (2). For Goodman, the two terms are synonymous. A workaholic is someone for whom work is a compulsion, one who takes the behavior of the workplace to an extreme, who never has a quitting time, and

who sacrifices everything in life for the sake of a job. Ask students about the suffix -*aholic;* where else have they seen it used?

2. The phrase "Important People" ironically implies those who spend all their time on work and work-related events, trying to acquire money, position, and power.

3. Goodman uses this selection to issue a warning to those who are in danger of falling prey to the same circumstances that eventually killed Phil. The cold, detached tone of the essay matches the cold, detached attitude of Phil toward what really should have been the most important things in his life—his wife and children.

4. Goodman's unemotional tone enhances the irony and sarcasm of the essay. Her diction of irony and sarcasm is encapsulated in her descriptions of Phil. She writes about how Phil acknowledged weekends by wearing a sports jacket to the office instead of a suit. He is described matter-of-factly, being "of course, overweight, by twenty or twenty-five pounds" (4). He always ate lunch—egg salad sandwiches—at his desk. Have your students find other examples of Goodman's sarcastic and ironic diction.

5. The time of Phil's death is repeated to drive home the irony that he died at 3:00 A.M. on a Sunday, a time when hardly anyone is working at all.

Classroom Activity Using Definition

This activity encourages students to explore how connotations work and how different people have different associations with some words. For example, some people think that a "go-getter" is a self-motivated, determined person, whereas others might see such a person as pushy, aggressive, or selfish. As writers, we all need to be aware of the connotations that our audience might bring to the words we use.

What Happiness Is (p. 456)
■ **Eduardo Porter**

Essay Analysis and Discussion

In addition to stressing the *kinds* of happiness, try also exploring what it takes to make people happy. Ask students to call out things that make them happy, and write them on the board. People have different rules for happiness. For some, it might be simply a blue sky; another may need a marriage proposal, straight A's, or a trophy. Happiness appears to have many health benefits; therefore, ought we spend our day looking for ways to be happy? For example, could happiness be found in the appreciation of something beautiful, say the Taj Mahal as described in Salman Rushdie's essay? You may want to point out that Porter's essay discusses "what happiness is" and the benefits, but not *how* to be happy. Do students think that this omission is an important missing element of the essay?

Thinking Critically about This Reading

Porter means that although people are able to make distinctions between temporary and long-term states of contentment, they tend to focus on instant satisfaction. Knowing the difference does not, he believes, lead to a change in behavior. Many students will agree that the allure of short-term satisfaction may be stronger than that of long-term happiness. Eating the cookie versus the fruit, smoking the cigarette versus going for a run, partying versus studying, watching TV versus practicing guitar, and spending money versus saving it are all examples that might be useful for students struggling with the question.

Questions for Study and Discussion

1. Porter demonstrates the variety of definitions of happiness by quoting various well-known figures on the subject. He quotes Gandhi, Lincoln, and Snoopy in paragraph 1. This beginning grabs readers' attention because Gandhi and Lincoln are commonly viewed as people worthy of respect and attention. The addition of Snoopy lightens the tone and attracts readers not drawn to the other readers. Each quote is thought provoking and distinct.

2. In paragraph 2, Porter introduces the three parts of subjective well-being: *satisfaction, positive feelings like joy,* and *the absence of negative feelings like anger.* Because happiness can have so many definitions, as described in paragraph 1, reviewing these subdivisions allows readers to juggle the multiple meanings and discuss them separately. These subdivisions also help readers consider and measure their own happiness on a variety of scales.

3. Happiness is related to quality of life in that happier people are healthier, have better relationships, and have a positive feeling about life. More specifically, they tend to be healthier (fewer colds, lower blood pressure), heal more quickly, smile more, sleep better, want to live, and claim to have happier relations (3).

4. In paragraph 7, Porter uses a story about Lincoln and a pig to make a point about happiness. Lincoln saves a pig from the mud for *his own* happiness. The point is that different people have different rules for happiness. Superior people and extraordinary people like Lincoln have linked happiness with the alleviation of suffering. This story challenges the reader to question what makes them happy and, on a deeper level, what shifts they could make so that reliving the suffering of others would be a part of that.

5. Porter introduces economics into the discussion by equating the economic term of "utility" with "happiness." He believes that we pursue what we think will make us happy, but disagrees with the argument that the pur-

suit of economic growth is the result of the pursuit of happiness. He says that too many people make decisions that are good for economic growth but not necessarily good for long-term happiness. Decisions that might serve economic growth but not happiness could be those, he says, that harm the environment. He says that people go for economic growth because they think that it will make them happy. A limitation with Porter's model could be that although he claims that people are pursuing happiness, they might really be pursuing financial security and significance, a feeling of importance. Focusing on security and significance through economic growth is not the same thing as focusing on love and connection, which arguably contribute far more to happiness. Not all wealthy cultures are happy. Students may also argue that happiness is a state of being rather than a pursuit.

Classroom Activity Using Definition

Student definitions will vary. Some possible definitions follow.

competition: a motivating force, opponent for limited resources, a sporting event, a negative emotion between friends.

wealth: greed, luck, the accumulation of money, access to the best of everything, financial security, financial freedom, a specific amount—say one million dollars.

success: achieving one's goals, achieving society's goals, happiness, wealth, professional accomplishment, recognition of others.

jerk: an uncaring or selfish person, a crude person, someone who steals parking spots, a liar, someone who lacks empathy or compassion.

superstar: someone recognized internationally for their accomplishments, anyone famous either from accomplishments or simply by birth, a game changer.

failure: inability to reach one's objectives, rejection, a grade on an exam or in a course, not living according to one's moral code, to be inadequate, bankruptcy.

poverty: lack of money, lack of access to clean water, health care, homelessness, starvation.

luxury: five-star hotels, fancy sheets, having time to do whatever one wants to do, vacation time, first-class travel, fine clothes, housekeeper or cook, something rare.

beauty: nature, a fit body, the way one moves, colorful, a flower, any sight, idea, or sound that moves someone or gratifies them, grace.

The Ways of Meeting Oppression (p. 465)
■ **Martin Luther King Jr.**

Essay Analysis and Discussion

In addition to being an excellent example of division and classification, King's essay is a model of how to achieve unity between paragraphs. To help students see the unity in this essay, have them identify the topic sentence in each of King's paragraphs and make a list of those statements. They should come up with the following:

1. "One way is acquiescence: the oppressed resign themselves to their doom."
2. "There is such a thing as the freedom of exhaustion."
3. "So acquiescence—while often the easier way—is not the moral way."
4. "A second way that oppressed people sometimes deal with oppression is to resort to physical violence and corroding hatred."
5. "Violence as a way of achieving racial justice is both impractical and immoral."
6. "Violence is not the way."
7. "The third way open to oppressed people in their quest for freedom is the way of nonviolent resistance."
8. "It seems to me that this is the method that must guide the actions of the Negro in the present crisis in race relations."
9. "Nonviolent resistance makes it possible for the Negro to remain in the South and struggle for his rights."
10. "By nonviolent resistance, the Negro can also enlist all men of good will in his struggle for equality."

This list demonstrates how tightly King's ideas are connected as he moves from paragraph to paragraph. The supporting information that surrounds these topic sentences explains and strengthens the main idea of each paragraph, but it is the close connection between those main ideas that gives the essay its unity and makes King's logical argument, and the presentation of the ways to meet oppression, so easy to follow and understand.

Thinking Critically about This Reading

The "freedom of exhaustion" refers to a kind of giving up that engulfs the slave to the extent that he does not even "mind" his slavery anymore, and if he does not mind, he is "free" to do nothing about it.

Questions for Study and Discussion

1. "Oppressed people deal with their oppression in three characteristic ways" (1).

2. King classifies the three types of oppression to create a logical progression from passivity to violence to his preferred method, nonviolent resistance.
3. King uses *climactic order* to illustrate the least to most effective tactics for meeting oppression.
4. He is able to clearly argue the inferiority of the first two ways before offering his preferred solution.
5. Acquiescence builds nothing for future generations. For King, violence is immoral and only begets more violence.

Classroom Activity Using Division and Classification

Ask students to explain in their own words the differences between division and classification. Next, ask them how they might apply these strategies to the real-life tasks listed in the exercise. For example, in searching for MP3s on the Web, students would naturally find it easier to narrow down their searches to the already-established genres of music that interest them. But students might also narrow a search based on other reasons. For example, they might rule out music they feel is "overplayed."

You can point out to students that division and classification both help us to organize ideas, facts, objects, and events. By grouping and dividing elements into sensible, meaningful categories and sub-categories, we can better understand, study, and write about complex topics. Dividing allows us to grasp and remember information that might otherwise be perceived of as undifferentiated or vague. The process of dividing (for example, types of literature, legislation, students, or retirees) into sub-groups allows us to make important and interesting distinctions that might otherwise avoid our notice. Classifying similarly allows us to group "like with like" and zero in on essential, defining characteristics (for example, among types of musical instruments, birds, businesses, or new technologies). Through both processes, classifying and dividing, we can become better attuned to nuances and to sometimes subtle yet crucial differences and similarities. On the flip side, dividing and classifying can be dangerous, leading to stereotyping or hasty generalizations. But thoughtfully undertaken, the processes can help us see helpful, underlying patterns. They can help us avoid a human tendency to lump things or people together—like stars and planets—into poorly defined categories on occasion, without necessarily a lot of thought or knowledge.

What Are Friends For? (p. 470)
■ **Marion Winik**

Essay Analysis and Discussion

Friendships and all relationships are often the place of greatest joy and greatest pain for people. Winik's light tone allows her to discuss friendships in a humorous way. She can encourage the reader to think about different types of friendships and different ways of relating without readers putting up their guard or getting defensive. Ask students to consider how their reaction to the essay might have been different had Winik used academic-sounding classifications. Would students have found more fault with her classifications?

Thinking Critically about This Reading

Winik is talking about male and female friends. She refers to "that special guy at work" (5). When discussing the Faraway Friend, she uses the female pronoun. With the Friends You Love to Hate and Hero Friends, she uses gender neutral language.

Questions for Study and Discussion

1. In the first paragraph, she introduces the idea that friends play different roles. She highlights the difference between the grocery line person and the friend whose shoulder one would cry on. Every reader could agree that there is a difference. Then, in later paragraphs, she moves to further distinctions.
2. Winik's purpose is to show the reader that we have different kinds of friends and that they play different roles in our lives. Knowing and understanding this fact helps us laugh at ourselves, appreciate these friends for their unique contributions, and maybe even consider what kind of friend we are being.
3. She illustrates the different types of friends by dedicating a section of the essay of each type. She reviews their behavior, role, and frequency with which one sees them. She also reviews the boundaries of each friendship. For example, she mentions knowing the names of a coworker's pets but not spending time together outside of work.
4. Friends You Love to Hate need you because they need help. They have many problems, and your attention and their belief that you love them keep them going.
5. With a New Friend, everything feels new. Your life story becomes interesting and fresh again, your perspectives are eagerly sought, and your faults are minimized.
6. Her tone is light. She uses funny references such as knowing the names of your coworker's turtles. This light tone allows her to simplify the friendship categories and describe them in broad strokes. Had she used a more academic or professional tone, readers would have more deeply considered the roles of different friendships and perhaps challenged her on less important points outside the scope of her purpose.

Classroom Activity Using Division and Classification

One way the figures can be grouped is into those with black ties, with bow ties, and with white ties. The subdivisions within each group are those with happy faces and with sad faces. You also may want to discuss the limitations and dangers of classifications. For example, stereotyping which applies certain characteristics to a group that may be shared by some, but not all, the group's members.

Doubts about Doublespeak (p. 477)
■ William Lutz

Essay Analysis and Discussion

Lutz's piece provides an excellent opportunity for examining the importance of examples in a particular type of essay. In this case, it is hard to imagine Lutz being able to make his point without emphasizing the role of examples. To a certain extent, the examples *are* the point. You can follow your discussion of Lutz's essay with a class activity that identifies other topics that would require extensive use of examples. Then select one of those topics and have students, either as a class or in small groups, generate the specific examples that would support it. Finally, have students arrive at a tentative thesis that their list of examples suggests to them and sketch out an organizational pattern appropriate for such a purpose. They might begin with Lutz's organizational scheme and consider the degree to which it generally fits this kind of essay.

Thinking Critically about This Reading

Lutz does not provide a specific plan for combating doublespeak, but he suggests that familiarizing ourselves with its various forms will help us see through the misleading fog of language to the true meaning hidden beneath. You might consider asking students—individually or in groups—to develop plans of their own for combating doublespeak.

Questions for Study and Discussion

1. Lutz presents his thesis at the beginning of paragraph 2: "Doublespeak is language which pretends to communicate but doesn't." The rest of paragraph 2 expands on and clarifies this statement. Lutz reiterates his thesis about midway through the essay, in paragraph 9.
2. The four kinds of doublespeak are euphemism, jargon, gobbledygook or bureaucratese, and inflated language. Lutz's organizational pattern is to identify the type of doublespeak, define it, describe its function or its consequences, and then provide examples to illustrate. His approach seems well-suited to his subject matter because he acquaints readers with the information necessary to fully appreciate the significance of the examples.
3. Lutz has used division and classification to explain the different classes of doublespeak.

4. Lutz has ordered his categories from least to most complex to demonstrate how complicated and obtuse doublespeak can be.

5. Students' opinions about the effectiveness of Lutz's examples may vary, but, chances are, they will find his illustrations representative of the kinds of doublespeak that they have encountered in their own lives. Whether they believe that Lutz could have used more or fewer examples may depend on their own familiarity with the different kinds of doublespeak. In an organizational sense, Lutz appears to effectively balance his examples with discussion and analysis of their significance.

6. Changing the order of the first two paragraphs would diminish the effectiveness of Lutz's beginning. Without the context provided by the examples in paragraph 1, the discussion in paragraph 2 would seem abrupt and uninviting. The examples themselves offer an engaging introductory subject matter, but their presentation also establishes a slightly humorous and ingratiating tone.

7. Students may well disagree on whether the serious claim at the end is justified by the body of Lutz's essay. On one hand, the sheer number of examples establishes the prominence of doublespeak as a phenomenon within our language. Lutz's discussion of what each kind of doublespeak intends to accomplish also supports his notion of how our perception of reality is altered. On the other hand, students may find some inconsistency between the humorous tone that underlies Lutz's discussion and the serious claim at the end.

Classroom Activity Using Division and Classification

Here are some possible classification criteria for the first group, Hobbies:

sports	sendentary activities
spectator sports	physical activities
participatory sports	

CHAPTER 19 **Comparison and Contrast**

Two Ways of Seeing a River (p. 488)
■ **Mark Twain**

Essay Analysis and Discussion

This selection from Mark Twain's *Life on the Mississippi* is remarkable for the way it shows how one's perception of something—in this case, Twain's perception of the river—can change with education. With Twain's knowledge of steamboat piloting comes the ability to differentiate between the "appearance" of the river and the "reality" of the river. What once appeared as "graceful circles and radiating lines" (paragraph 1) on the river's surface are now for Twain "a warning that that troublesome place is shoaling up dangerously" (2). Extend the discussion of Twain's experience to other arenas, and ask students to share times when knowledge has changed their views of something.

Thinking Critically about This Reading

The appearance of the river is one of beauty, poetry, and grace in the first paragraph, but in the second paragraph Mark Twain describes the reality of the river. Now that he works on the river, he sees the river in a practical way, translating previously ethereal images into guidelines used by steamboaters.

Questions for Study and Discussion

1. Block organization is used in this essay. The only other option in a comparison and contrast selection would be a point-by-point organization, which would involve quickly and frequently going back and forth between the two views to show specific examples. This quick alternation would ruin the narrative flow.

2. The analogy of a doctor being unable to appreciate human beauty because he or she has gained too much knowledge about the practicalities of human beings and their illnesses is effective and appropriate. In addition, by providing an example that is vastly different from his own experience—doctor and steamboater—Twain shows the reader a broad spectrum of examples. The reader realizes that, with almost everything, the acquisition of knowledge comes at the cost of losing an elemental—and innocent—response to beauty.

3. "Long, ruffled trail," "shone like silver," "boiling tumbling rings . . . as many-tinted as an opal," and "splendor that was flowing from the sun" are examples of simile and metaphor found in this essay. Have your students find others—the entire paragraph 2 directly compares and contrasts with the views expressed in paragraph 1.

4. According to Twain, there are two ways to see the river, but one option is removed once the river becomes his place of "business." Becoming an adept steamboater was a triumph for Twain, but there was a trade-off: "I had made a valuable acquisition. But I had lost something, too . . . which could never be restored to me. . . . All the grace, the beauty, the poetry, had gone out of the majestic river!" (1).

5. Mark Twain feels that the practical, detailed knowledge he gains as a steamboat pilot creates a barrier between him and his former ability to see beauty and feel "rapture" when looking at the river. The knowledge, in his mind, is in the role of a block, an obstruction, or even an active destroyer

of his formerly joyful appreciation of the romance of the river. To him, the analytical way of seeing, knowing, and deciphering visual data destroys the elevating and transporting way of seeing powerful poetic or holistic impressions. He recognizes that technical knowledge is essential for him to do his job, just as medical knowledge is essential for a doctor, to diagnose and cure illness. But in both cases, he feels that gaining this experience, expertise, and in-depth knowledge means sacrificing the capacity to see "the glories and charms" (paragraph 2) of the river with the old appreciation and wonder. Twain presents the matter as an either/or situation. Either one is uninformed or untutored on the nitty-gritty facts of the river but able to be innocently enraptured by it, or one is informed and expert on the facts—thus able to do a good job as a pilot—but then not able to be enraptured by the views and vistas seen on the river. For him, knowledge represents paradise lost.

Classroom Activity Using Comparison and Contrast

For this exercise, it might be interesting to ask students who picked the same topic to get into groups together. In these groups, they can explain how they organized the outlines. It will be interesting to see how much variety exists even when people choose the same topic. This exercise can help students see how many options they have.

Two Ways to Belong in America (p. 493)
■ Bharati Mukherjee

Essay Analysis and Discussion

Mukherjee and her sister both moved to the United States seeking an education. They both embraced a life in the States. While they chose to live outside of their home nation, marry the man of their choice (rather than of their family's choosing), and prosper professionally in the United States, they reacted differently to "being American." Mukherjee embraced her new nation, marrying an American and becoming a citizen. Her sister, however, maintained her immigrant status, married an Indian, and maintained a sense of her Indian self. While the sisters remained close, they were divided by their differing views on immigration and both were dramatically affected by the governing laws around them. Both have been hurt and disgruntled. The main difference between the two women's experiences is that the author transformed herself into an American, hoping this change would distinguish her from other "immigrants." Her sister escaped the pain of transformation in exchange for remaining somewhat an outsider and constant representative of her homeland.

Thinking Critically about This Reading

Mukherjee's sister wishes that the United States' new laws affecting legal immigrants be applied only to those who arrive once the laws are in place, not before. She feels like she was taunted here, even though she paid her taxes and contributed to society. Then, when the government felt like changing the laws, it lumped her in with other immigrants. The sister felt useful in the eyes of the government only when it served the latter's political purposes, regardless of her contributions. So she says that she would become a citizen in name only, converting back to her native citizenship when she returned to India. She will become a citizen just to play the game rather than because of any real intention to become American. She will "use" the country the way it "used" her.

Questions for Study and Discussion

1. Mukherjee's thesis is that although two immigrants may be almost identical in terms of background and life choices, one's approach to immigrant status leads to pronounced differences in how one assimilates into the new environment.

2. Mukherjee uses a point-by-point pattern to compare and contrast herself with her sister.

3. This point-by-point pattern works well because sisters in general, and these sisters in particular, have so many physical and cultural links. They are like one person at the beginning, and it is best to look at them together to see the subtleties and complexities of their differences. You almost have to unwind one from the other to see how the experience of immigrating to a new country could be a rebirth for one and a cultural experience for the other. Even though these differences emerge, the point-by-point comparison enables Mukherjee to show how both were angered by the immigration legislation that affected their experiences. This method also works well for sisters who constantly compare themselves with each other. They don't evaluate themselves separately as one might two different baseball teams. Each sees herself reflected in the other.

4. The essay starts with the similarities and moves into their differences and then back into their similarities. Mukherjee wanted to show the parallels of their beginnings in India, their hopes and agendas in the United States, and the early stages of their years in there. They both had planned to leave, and both stayed. Only as the years they were in the United States added up did their differences emerge. We then see how they approached assimilation and even their shared frustration.

5. Mukherjee argues that by assimilating you get closer to both the "mythic depths or the superficial pop culture of this society" (7). Also, long-term legal immigrants have been facing increasing scrutiny, and new laws make it harder for even long-term residents to feel that they are welcome guests.

If you don't want to feel used, she believes, you have to join the team. You have to spend your time maintaining an identity and defending yourself. Citizens often dump long-term immigrants into the same category as new immigrants, making it harder for the former to be accepted and appreciated for years of contributions. Mira argues that if she obeys all the rules, pays her taxes, and does her job well, she deserves to be treated with respect and allowed to maintain her cultural ties. Mira feels what she calls an irrational attachment to India that she believes she deserves to maintain. She thinks that by maintaining this connection she can have a certain structure and sense of self that Mukherjee had to release to be transformed.

6. Her sister feels used by the changing laws because she worked and paid taxes all those years and all of a sudden is being treated as if she has just arrived. She believes that she contributed to the culture and was an asset to the country. This feeling is especially pronounced since she has been nationally recognized for her work. The new laws act as if none of those contributions matter, as if all that matters is that she is an immigrant.

7. Mukherjee claims that many people like her sister have been able to come to the United States and maintain their cultural identities. To a great degree they have been able to avoid the pain of assimilation. To truly immigrate means releasing an old self and giving birth to a new one. She finds this process stressful and often jolting. She wants the reader to understand that becoming a citizen is not an easy experience emotionally, which is perhaps why so many, like her sister, avoid it.

Classroom Activity Using Comparison and Contrast

Discuss with students how they chose the figures or leaders that they chose to compare. On what did they base this comparison? Now ask them if they think, after completing this exercise, that they would be able to find enough material to write an entire paper. Students may find that although they have chosen well-known figures, they will not have enough to say about these figures for an essay. Discuss with students what characteristics need to be present for a successful comparison-contrast.

That Lean and Hungry Look (p. 499)
■ Suzanne Britt

Essay Analysis and Discussion

This essay, while criticizing skinny people, is not insulting. Ask students how Britt's word choice and tone allow her to write a sensitive topic that is not, to most people, alienating. They can underline and share several expressions they find funny that lighten the tone. For example, she starts the essay with a reference to Caesar's serious character, which could throw off the reader. The second line immediately changes the tone. Caesar is not usually quoted for his comments on thin people. She also really sets the tone at the end of paragraph 1 when she says that all thin people are dangerous. Clearly they are not. Saying untrue things also allows her to offer true insights without insulting thin readers.

Thinking Critically about This Reading

Britt seems to be against thin people's constant desire to be constantly productive, efficient, and on the move. She thinks that they are dangerous because they are not fun and do not know how to enjoy life. Because she is so critical of thin people and complimentary of fat people, readers can assume that Britt herself is a larger woman.

Questions for Study and Discussion

1. She uses a point-by-point pattern. She discusses different qualities of thin people and compares those qualities to fat people. A subject-by-subject approach would have been to discuss thin people in one section of the essay and then switch completely to fat people. She discusses thin people's constant need to be doing something, then their belief in logic, and finally their oppressiveness and inability to be fun.

2. She characterizes thin people as efficient, speedy, oppressive, logical, mathematical, and moral. She characterizes fat people as "sluggish, inert, easygoing" (paragraph 3) and able to have fun.

3. Her purpose is to present a humorous essay that points out to readers that there is value in not being so perfectly efficient and logical all the time. She advocates for being able to relax and enjoy life at a slower pace. In this sense, her essay is more about efficiency versus enjoyment, not about fat versus thin.

4. There are four examples in this essay of sentences with three words or less:

    a. "Caesar was right" (1), which alludes to Shakespeare's famous line, serves to catch her reader's attention in an efficient way.

    b. "I disagree" (4). This sentence works as a short, emphatic rebuttal to the sentence that precedes it.

    c. "They know better" (5). This sentence clarifies the meaning of the sentence before it, and the two work together to refute thin people's belief in logic, which the rest of paragraph 5 develops.

    d. "Phrases like that" (7). After listing the phrases that thin people "spout," Britt seems to wink at the reader, as if to say, "You know what I mean."

5. Although clichés are overused and tired expressions, they evoke the predictable mental associations. Britt relies on these associations to help draw

out the personalities of the two "types" she describes. Also, these clichés add to the cartoon-like nature of her descriptions. All thin and fat people, of course, do not fall into these categories; they are oversimplified descriptions, and the clichés help Britt oversimplify. Clichés themselves are simple broad strokes, just like her descriptions. In doing so, she makes the essay light, humorous, and accessible. Twelve examples of clichés in her essay are the following:

"there aren't enough hours in the day" (2)   "fit as a fiddle" (7)
"problems to tackle" (3)   "ducks in a row" (7)
"to the heart of the matter" (4)   "neat as a pin" (10)
"face the truth" (4)   "cry in your beer" (12
"the key thing" (4)   "put your name in the pot" (12)
"get a grip on yourself" (7)   "let you off the hook" (12)

6. She uses alliteration in the last paragraph. She describes fat people as folks who will "gab, giggle, guffaw, galumph, gyrate, and gossip" (12). She adds they can also be "generous, giving and gallant . . . gluttonous and goodly and great" (12). Alliteration is fun, childlike, and playful, like the image she wants to create of fat people.

Classroom Activity Using Comparison and Contrast

Ambrose organizes the paragraph by the subjects' common traits, but he also explains just how different the two were. His goal was to show how similar Custer and Crazy Horse were, but for different reasons. For example, he points out that both Custer and Crazy Horse set themselves apart from their crowd, but Custer did so by being flamboyant and Crazy Horse did so by being reserved. These details speak volumes not only about the subjects, but about the communities that they came from. Had Ambrose organized the paragraphs differently, the differences between the pair would have most likely been the focus, rather than the traits that they shared.

Who Says a Woman Can't Be Einstein? (p. 505)
■ Amanda Ripley

Essay Analysis and Description

This article takes a scientific look at the differences between men and women. An interesting comparison would be with the Marion Winik article, "What Are Friends For?" in which she reviews different types of friends in a much more colloquial manner. Ask the students to compare and contrast the articles in terms of the tone. Do they take Ripley's analysis more seriously? If so, why? Sometimes light and humorous articles can be more effective. Why might Ripley have chosen this straight-forward approach? Answers might include that the tones are appropriate to the subject. Because Ripley's essay responds to ideas presented in an academic setting regarding academic performance, a professional tone is more appropriate. As a woman, she also wants to make the point that *she* can be as intelligent as the men writing on the subject. Winik's article about friendship is written in a tone more likely to be used among friends. An academic tone would have been off-putting. Friends rarely speak to each other the way Ripley writes.

Thinking Critically about This Reading

Ripley presents studies and statistics that show that although there may be biological differences, scientific conclusions keep evolving, various environmental factors affect performance, and the brain differences fail to explain the increasing success of female students around the world. Conclusions about the size of the corpus callosum changed between the 19th and 20th centuries (paragraph 9). Scientists still cannot distinguish brains by gender (10). Studies conducted at Temple University using the video game Tetris showed that woman could improve spatially and even surpass the men without too much effort. This research shows that practice can overcome biological differences. Ripley also cites the increasing success of female students around the world in algebra, university attendance, and their decreased reports of conditions like attention deficit disorder. This situation is therefore complex, and any surface conclusions, Ripley believes, can be dangerous and misleading.

Questions for Study and Discussion

1. Ripley opens her essay presenting Summers's remarks on gender disparities as "something self-destructive." Using the expression "self-destructive" allows Ripley herself to be as provocative as Summers and hook the reader into her essay.

2. Ripley organizes her essay into the following four lessons.

    1. LESSON 1: Function over Form. This section reviews the differences in brain architecture between the genders.
    2. LESSON 2: The Segregation of the Senses. Men and women tend to instinctively rely on certain senses over others. Men focus on movement and women on color and texture. This difference appears to have survival value.
    3. LESSON 3: Never Underestimate the Brain. This lesson supports the view that while differences exist, changes in environment can compensate.
    4. LESSON 4: Expectations Matter. Because personality and discipline have such an impact on success we ought to be careful of assuming attributes based on biology. Women succeed globally in math and

science. It would be dangerous to assume based on findings that they ought not to pursue those fields.

These divisions help Ripley organize and highlight the complexity of the differences. What Summers throws out as a conclusive statement is broken down by Ripley's four-part analysis. Students may or may not have appreciated the four-part division in their first reading.

3. Men's brains tend to be 10% bigger than women's and although men are on average 8% taller than women, there still remains a slight brain size difference. Women have more connections between the two hemispheres, they tend to use more parts of their brains to accomplish certain tasks, and they have stronger connections between the amygdala and the language center of the brain. Brain functions relating to verbal fluency, handwriting, and face recognition mature faster in girls than in boys; the area of spatial reasoning matures faster in boys than in girls.

4. Lesson 2 begins with the following two questions: Why are men better at rotating 3-D objects in their mind, and why do girls and women have stronger verbal skills and social sensitivity? She answers these questions by stating that different genders rely more heavily on certain senses and thus practice early focusing on what they see. If boys and men are programmed to look for movement, it makes sense that they want to play with moving objects like trucks and observe mobiles. If girls and women prefer color and texture, other activities might please them.

5. The rhesus monkey research provided insight and evidence for male spatial strengths. That research also showed, however, that as the monkeys aged the differences lessened, suggesting that time plays a role. The research on rats examined retinas and showed a biological reason why men might be focused on motion and women prefer texture and color. In the men-as-hunters and females-as-gatherers gender division, such a difference would be useful.

6. For every supposed difference she highlights, Ripley cites a source. She uses citations to distinguish herself from Summers, who simply made a strong statement, and to give herself credibility.

   a. In paragraph 4, she integrates Sandra Witelson's comment about the brain as a sex organ as an overarching comment for the essay.

   b. She quotes Yu Xie in paragraph 6 to emphasize the point that although biological differences are important, environmental factors have a significant impact. Xie's perspective holds most closely to Ripely's own.

   c. Richard Haier takes the biology point one step further in paragraph 8 and adds what Ripley calls *imagination* to the situation. He believes that if something is biologically determined, it can also be biologically altered. For him, the differences and the origin of those differences create opportunity, not limitations. This view seems to be distinct from

Summers's, whose comment suggested that biology made things so—end of discussion, from Summers's view.

    d.   She integrates Leonard Sax in paragraph 26 to discuss sensory differences. His studies make up the brunt of her second and third lessons.

    e.   In paragraph 27, she quotes psychiatrist Jay Giedd to emphasize the remarkable ability to change. This quotation helps her make the point that while biology determines emphasis, the situation is not immutable.

    f.   Nora Newcombe is cited in paragraph 28 to demonstrate when such change has been possible. Her study is integrated to support Giedd's hypothesis.

    g.   Paragraph 32 refers to a book by Kim Tolley. Tolley's work is integrated to show the impressive performance over boys in the sciences.

7.   Sax's perspective is in the middle, writes Ripley: "Boys and girls are innately different and . . . we must change the environment so differences don't become limitations" (24). He supports having separate classes for boys and girls.

Classroom Activity Using Comparison and Contrast

The most important differences between a cold and H1N1 flu are the following:

- Colds offer a productive cough, flus produce an unproductive cough.
- Colds lead to slight body aches, flus to severe aches and pains.
- A stuffy nose is usually present only in a cold.
- Sneezing is associated with colds, not with flus.
- Sore throat is common with colds, not with flus.

People often confuse colds and flus because they have many similar characteristics. Most students will find the chart helpful and informative. They might find it surprising that sore throats, stuffy noses, and sneezing are not associated with the flu. Some might suggest that there be a third column that has a check mark in rows where symptoms are shared, even if differing in severity; or highlighting or putting a marker where they are different.

CHAPTER 20 **Cause and Effect**

The Famine of Bengal (p. 521)
■ Gita Mehta

Essay Analysis and Discussion

This essay's strength is its ability to communicate a great deal in just a few paragraphs. Ask students how Mehta is able to accomplish all she does in a short space. Many essays of greater length are less descriptive and powerful. What would have been lost if she had gone into the details of the ruling powers and measures by the government to alleviate the famine? By focusing on the simultaneous extreme presence and absence of food, she is able to focus the reader's attention, both intellectually and emotionally.

Thinking Critically about This Reading

Britain was administering aid to India during the time of the famine. The British scorched crops near the Burmese border to prevent the Japanese from having access in the event of an invasion. A cyclone in 1942 caused floods, which ruined crops and forced the people to eat their surplus. Nobel Prize–winner Amartya Sen argues that it was not the floods and scorching that ultimately led to the three-million-person famine, but the delay in official response. He claimed that shortage rumors led to hoarding and price inflation, which ended the easy circulation of food. Combined with wage cuts, laborers and other nonlandowners were not able to afford food. Apparently, the government of Bengal made efforts to rectify the situation by introducing free trade for rice in India, on the eastern side, in the hopes that this policy would help the Bengalis. It was unsuccessful. The British military made efforts to reduce the famine. They were able to successfully deliver 110,000,000 meals that, although significant, could not save the three million people. The famine ended when the government based in London shipped grain to Bengal. Because this method was successful, we have reason to believe that the famine could have been ended far earlier.

Questions for Study and Discussion

1. Mehta's purpose is to highlight the needless death of three million people caused by famine and relate it to the current hunger problem in the United States. Although she does not mention the United States until the final line, the last paragraph is stated in general terms to show that an injustice on the scale of what happened in India is slowly happening today.

2. The immediate cause of the famine, according to Mehta, was the farmers' decision to immediately sell all their grain demanded for the expected armies. They hoped that this selling would free them of debt.

3. The ultimate causes of the famine were the middlemen who ended up controlling the food and controlling the prices, as well as the lack of immediate and effective intervention on the part of the British government to end the black market.

4. Black marketeering is the control of the sale of goods by a handful of people who set prices illegally instead of letting the market determine the price. Having control over the entire supply allows black marketeers to control the price. The English government, distracted by war, and the local officials disempowered by colonial leadership both allowed the black marketeering to continue uninterrupted for too long.

5. Her last line encourages readers to consider the hunger today in the United States and to take action to alleviate the suffering. Mehta does not say that the problem in the United States today is as extreme as the famine in Bengal in the 1940s. What she does point out, however, is how the lack of caring even today in a prosperous country allows this suffering to continue needlessly.

Classroom Activity Using Cause and Effect

Fire drill/fear

Ultimate Cause: Safety regulation requires fire drills.
Immediate Cause: Alarms sound.
Effect: People in the building hear the alarm and react.
Effect: People feel frightened by the sound of the alarm, not knowing if it is a drill or a real fire.

Giving a speech/anxiety

Ultimate Cause: A speech is required.
Immediate Cause: Going up on stage in front of a group of people.
Effect: Feeling anxious on stage.

Party/excitement

Ultimate Cause: Invitation has been received to attend a party.
Immediate Cause: Getting dressed for the party, making plans for transportation, talking to friends.
Effect: Excitement regarding the event.

Vacation/relaxation

Ultimate Cause: Days off from work or school closed.
Immediate Cause: Time off from homework and responsibility.
Effect: Relaxation.

New Exercise Schedule/Increased Fitness

Ultimate Cause: Signed up for a marathon.
Immediate Cause: A new workout schedule.
Effect: Fitness increased.

Why We Crave Horror Movies (p. 524)
■ **Stephen King**

Essay Analysis and Discussion

In his first sentence, King tells us that we are all mentally ill, then he suggests that our love of horror movies helps us feel balanced because those movies provide a psychic release for our darker feelings. In paragraphs 8 through 10, King defines the nature of our insanity in more detail and explains how society forces us to deal with our darker emotions. Next, King suggests that because we cannot flaunt our meaner feelings, we need an outlet for them, through horror movies and the "sick" joke. He has gone through his argument twice, with more emphasis on explaining the nature of our illness the second time through. He presents a thesis—that we are all mentally ill—and then carefully uses our love of horror movies and the sick joke to prove it. The horror movie gives us permission to express our dark feelings; those dark feelings are forbidden; they are forbidden because they are "crazy." Can students refute King's position using a cause-and-effect argument of their own? Or is he right?

Thinking Critically about This Reading

The horror movie maintains the status quo of the nature of good and evil and beauty and ugliness in our minds. It does not ask us to rework our values.

Questions for Study and Discussion

1. We crave horror movies to show that we are not afraid, to reestablish our feelings of being normal, and to have fun. Some people go to satisfy a morbid curiosity about how the horror will be effected or because they are aficionados of the macabre.

2. King compares the thrills and chills of the roller-coaster ride with the thrills and chills of the horror movie. Each propels you along, promising to reward your terror at the next turn; and each fulfills that promise, but when you least expect it.

3. Society applauds love, friendship, loyalty, and kindness because they "maintain the status quo of civilization itself" (paragraph 9). King labels emotions that are mean and murderous as "anticivilization."

4. The sick joke and the horror movie both must appeal "to all that is worst in us" (12).

5. King gives examples of strange behavior that occurs in us all, moving from the innocence of people who talk to themselves to the potentially murderous lyncher. His last line suggests, as Freud did, that a darker, more menacing creature lies in wait beneath the civilized exterior we present to the world.

6. King's tone is humorously menacing. He, like the horror movie, likes to lead the viewer along and then without warning spring at the viewer with a grisly thought or a shocking idea. His first and final sentences are meant to bring the reader up short. In between, students will find numerous examples: "If your insanity leads you to carve up women" (8); "The potential lyncher is in almost all of us" (9); "But if we deliberately slam the rotten little puke of a sister's fingers in the door, sanctions follow" (10). King goes so far as to repeat for us one of the more horrifying of the "sick" jokes.

Classroom Activity Using Cause and Effect

This activity, which our first-year students have found eye-opening, is useful in demonstrating for your students how easy it is while reading to make assumptions that are based on little or no evidence. The activity is also useful in alerting the writer to the care that must be taken not to imply more than he or she knows.

Answers:

1. T   4. T   7. ?
2. ?   5. ?   8. F
3. ?   6. ?   9. ?

Why and When We Speak Spanish in Public (p. 531)
■ Myriam Marquez

Essay Analysis and Discussion

Marquez explains why she and her family sometimes speak Spanish, arguing that they are just as much American as anyone else. You may want to ask students whether they agree with Marquez. Is speaking English an important aspect of being an American? What are the reasons for speaking English in the United States? For example, how does English enable people to both assimilate and contribute more productively to the American culture and economy? Is it hard to give back if you cannot participate?

Thinking Critically about This Reading

In paragraph 11, Marquez lists the contributions Latin American immigrants have made to the United States: fighting in U.S.-led wars, voting, holding political office, and paying taxes. She argues that participation, not necessarily assimilation, is what makes someone an American.

Questions for Study and Discussion

1. Marquez's thesis is that speaking Spanish, rather than English, with her family is a way of acknowledging her roots and respecting her elders and is not in any way meant to denigrate the United States. "Being an American has very little to do with what language we use during our free time in a free country" (paragraph 7).

2. At several points, Marquez states the argument that she will refute. For example, in paragraph 5, she writes that she does not mean to be rude and, in paragraph 7, that being American does not require speaking English. She acknowledges that she understands the importance of English around

the world and also the importance of immigrants. Each paragraph is a refutation of an argument she has heard against immigrants' not speaking English.

3. She uses *but* to stress that she's challenging the point made in the preceding paragraph, in which she summarized an argument against speaking Spanish in an English-speaking country. Her use of *but* tempers the prior paragraph, while acknowledging the reality.

4. The essay is one of cause and effect. Marquez begins by saying that she speaks Spanish with her family and then explains why she does so.

5. Student opinion will vary. Consider asking students to discuss why they think that the founders did not make English the official language of the United States. Other countries have such laws—why not the United States?

Classroom Activity Using Cause and Effect

Causal chains can be confusing at first, and it is often difficult to distinguish between the ultimate cause, the immediate cause, and one or more of the effects when first developing the chain. It would probably help students to develop some chains as a class before they attempt to do so on their own. Take 15 to 20 minutes and have the students work together to come up with causal chains that are relevant to their own lives; then have them take another 10 minutes or so to develop one on their own.

Stuck on the Couch (p. 535)
■ Sanjay Gupta

Essay Analysis and Discussion

Gupta discusses why we stop exercising and how we can start again. He claims that a major life change such as going to college, getting married, or starting a new job is often used as an excuse to stop exercising. Setting concrete targets helps people get off the couch and start moving again, enabling them to have healthier lives.

Thinking Critically about This Reading

Student answers will vary. Some might say that they agree, having used starting college as an excuse to stop exercising. Recognizing that they have used this excuse, they might start again. Others might see college as an opportunity to be even more fit. They might be on sports teams or find a new running or tennis partner, for example. Others may say that they did stop exercising and that nothing other than a huge, mean coach will ever get them off the couch.

Questions for Study and Discussion

1. Gupta's purpose is to help people understand why they stop exercising and therefore encourage them to start again.

2. According to Bray, students stop exercising because academic demands increase and there is a lack of organized sports.

3. Herbert means that we spend much of our time exercising our self-control—at work, with children, and dieting. We get tired of trying to be good all the time and ultimately let things go. We might be too tired of following our own rules by the end of the day to then have to force ourselves to exercise.

4. Research has shown that over time having a personal trainer loses its effectiveness. People start to rely on the trainer instead of developing their own relationship to their exercise. We need to develop our own plan in addition to one we develop with a trainer. Simply remembering to sit up straight or drink enough water will help us build up our self-control muscle, encouraging us to stick to our fitness plans.

5. Set up a plan that is specific and achievable. For example, decide that you will walk to your friend's house on Monday, Wednesday, and Friday rather than make a general goal of "I will exercise more in my free time."

6. Student opinions will vary. Gupta writes casually, even though he uses references. Some students might want him to use a more professional tone. Others might want him to speak more colloquially.

Classroom Activity Using Cause and Effect

One of the difficult things about writing a cause-and-effect essay is that the effects are felt on many levels. The effect something has on you may not be at all the same as the effect it has on your neighbor, and it may affect society in ways that few people stop to think about in their daily lives. You can preface this activity with a discussion with your students about the effects of another recent innovation that has swiftly become an important part of our society—cell phones. Have students identify the different effects cell phones have had on individuals, communities, and society as a whole.

CHAPTER 21 **Argument**

The Declaration of Independence (p. 547)
■ Thomas Jefferson

Essay Analysis and Discussion

This essay can work well in conjunction with Abraham Lincoln's "Gettysburg Address" (copies readily available online, on Wikipedia and other sites) as an analysis of parallel sentence structure. The instances of parallelism in Lincoln's essay are accomplished either through repetition of word order within a single sentence or repetition of grammatical form in a series of sentences that make up one paragraph. Jefferson also relies on repetition of grammatical form, but develops the parallelism through a series of sentences, each of which serves as a paragraph in itself. Jefferson covers more ground than Lincoln, and his essay has a different purpose than Lincoln's essay. Have your students compare how the two types of parallelism are incorporated into these essays, and then discuss what effect the use of parallelism has on each. Lincoln's subtle and sonorous sentence structure, as opposed to Jefferson's more forceful and emphatic repetitions, may indicate the difference in tone between a dedication and a declaration.

Thinking Critically about This Reading

Government has power "to levy War, conclude Peace, contract Alliances, establish Commerce, and to do all other Acts and Things which Independent states may of right do" (paragraph 32). Students' responses as to what other purposes government may serve should show some understanding of the reasoning behind the Declaration of Independence. How do their recommendations differ from or agree with its basic concepts?

Questions for Study and Discussion

1. The self-evident truths that Jefferson puts forth in paragraph 2 are "all men are created equal," "they are endowed by their Creator with certain unalienable Rights," governments are instituted to secure these unalienable rights, and people have a right to throw off a despotic government. Once these truths are accepted, all the rest of Jefferson's argument follows logically.

2. Jefferson's argument can be stated in the following syllogism: *(major premise)* When a government is despotic it should be abolished and a new one established; *(minor premise)* the government of King George is despotic; *(conclusion)* the government of King George should be abolished and a new one established.

3. The major premise is presented as the consequence of self-evident truths and, as such, does not need to be supported.

4. In paragraph 31, Jefferson reviews the ways in which the colonies have attempted to make the British government aware of their problems.

5. The best examples of Jefferson's use of parallelism are found in paragraph 2, where he lists the unalienable rights, and in paragraphs 3 through 29, where he gives the charges against the king. Jefferson uses parallelism for emphasis; it establishes a rhythm that highlights each of the items in these lists, thus making the lists and the items memorable.

6. Examples of Jefferson's emotionally charged language include *wholesome* (3), *refused* (5), *inestimable* (5), *formidable* (5), *tyrants* (5), *manly* (7),

invasions (7), *swarms* (12), and *harass* (12). Having established a sound logical argument, Jefferson uses emotionally charged language to call forth feelings of patriotism among the colonists.

Classroom Activity Using Argument

This exercise works well as a group activity. Before setting students free on one of the suggested topics or a topic of your own choosing, make sure that they understand the dog leash law and waste pickup ordinance example provided in the text. This exercise gets students to focus on the essential pieces of an argument—in this case, three key points in favor of the writer's position (two logical and one emotional) and one point held by the opposition. After 15 to 20 minutes, have several groups write their key points on the board or present their thoughts orally.

I Have a Dream (p. 553)
■ **Martin Luther King Jr.**

Essay Analysis and Discussion

The classroom activity for this essay refers to the variety of metaphors King uses in his speech. King's reliance on figurative language is pervasive, and his metaphors often appear in a parallel structure that contributes to the rhetorical flourish of the speech overall. Notice, for example, the final sentence in paragraph 1: "It came as a joyous daybreak to end the long night of captivity." Day and night are coupled in the metaphor to highlight contrasting circumstances. King follows this pattern in many of his metaphors. In paragraph 2, "a lonely island of poverty" exists within "a vast ocean of material prosperity." The following are more examples of King's technique:

> "insufficient funds"/"great vaults of opportunity" (4)
> "desolate valley of segregation"/"sunlit path of racial justice" (4)
> "sweltering summer of the Negro's legitimate discontent"/"invigorating autumn of freedom and equality" (5)
> "warm threshold"/"palace of justice" (6)
> "desert state sweltering with the heat of injustice and oppression"/"oasis of freedom and justice" (13)
> "mountain of despair"/"stone of hope" (19)
> "jangling discords of our nation"/"beautiful symphony of brotherhood" (19)

Consider these examples as you examine King's more obvious parallel sentence structures (see question 4 on page 120 of this manual). Ask your students if they find the persistent metaphorical flourishes effective or if they believe that such flourishes become overwhelming as the essay proceeds.

Thinking Critically about This Reading

By warning against "wrongful deeds," King is responding to a growing militancy within the civil rights movement. Groups such as the Nation of Islam and leaders such as Malcolm X advocated a more aggressive, confrontational approach to gaining equality and did not rule out the use of violence if violence were directed at them. The more militant groups also believed that freedom and equality had to be fought for and won by African Americans themselves, without the aid of white sympathizers. King therefore wishes to emphasize his commitment to nonviolence and to integration in the battle for civil rights, fearing that any other approach could only be counterproductive in the long run.

Questions for Study and Discussion

1. King states his thesis at the beginning of paragraph 3: "In a sense we have come to our nation's Capitol to cash a check." He goes on to explain how the Constitution and the Declaration of Independence promised freedom and equality for every American, yet the United States has defaulted on that promise, as evidenced by continuing racial injustice, by segregation, by the lack of opportunity for African Americans—in short, by the denial of freedom and equality.

2. The larger audience for King's speech comprises everyone who listened to it on radio or watched it on television, either at the time it was given or at any time over the years since King presented it in 1963. In many ways, King's speech also addresses posterity, signaling a period of momentous change in U.S. history and reminding those who come after him of the circumstances that created the need for such a pivotal event. The repetitions and parallel structures within King's speech catch the audience's attention and make clear his argument.

3. After King's opening, in which he refers to the promise of the Emancipation Proclamation, King highlights the degree to which that promise has remained unfulfilled. He identifies the purpose of the gathering he addresses and presents his thesis in paragraph 3. The next stage in his argument emphasizes the need for demanding freedom and equality *now* and reminds the audience of African Americans' determination to secure citizenship rights. After cautioning against succumbing to bitterness and hatred, or "wrongful deeds," in the pursuit of equality, King then outlines some of the reasons why African Americans will not be satisfied until they are accorded their full rights as citizens. Next, King acknowledges the "trials and tribulations" that have brought people to Washington to protest,

using that acknowledgment to set up his extended refrain of "I have a dream . . ." in paragraphs 10 through 18. He then finishes with a rhetorical hymn for freedom.

King's organization suits his purpose overall, because the first part of his speech pays homage to the people who have gathered in Washington and acknowledges the conditions that have brought them there, whereas the second part finishes on a rhetorical high note full of hope and optimism, with the extended refrains of "I have a dream . . ." and "Let freedom ring. . . ."

4. The primary repetitions and parallel structures that appear in King's speech include the following:

one hundred years later . . . (2)
Now is the time . . . (4)
We can never be satisfied as long as . . . (7)
Some of you have come . . . (8)
Go back to . . . (9)
I have a dream . . . (11–18)
Let freedom ring . . . (21–26)

These structures add to the persuasiveness of King's argument in two key ways. First, they make more memorable the ideas he presents, emphasizing through repetition the most important points of his argument. Second, each time King uses one of the phrases above, he connects it to something specific concerning the conditions of African Americans in the United States or, in the case of *"Let freedom ring,"* how pervasive such conditions remain. Thus, at the same time that he reinforces the main points of his argument, he analyzes the nature of the problem he is addressing.

5. King's title emphasizes the spirit of hope and optimism that his speech engenders in the civil rights movement. It is particularly appropriate for the context in which the speech was given, because King verbalizes what is most likely the dream of all those present for the March on Washington in 1963. Students may have other opinions to offer on the suitability of King's title, as well as on possible alternatives.

Classroom Activity Using Argument

To choose the best quote for their paragraph, students will need to decide if they will use mostly persuasive arguments, logical arguments, or a mix of the two. The first quote will fit a mostly persuasive argument, the second a logical argument (let students know that they can make up other statistics if they wish), and the third can be used for both. Make sure that students integrate the quote into the paragraph so that it directly supports the argument and suits the tone. Students may enjoy reading their finished paragraphs aloud; have them discuss which method of presenting the argument is the most effective for each subject.

What Pro Sports Owners Owe Us (p. 560)
■ Dave Zirin

Essay Analysis and Discussion

You may want to discuss with the class different solutions to the problem Zirin puts forward. Instead of arguing that the teams owe fans respect, what if the fans abandoned expensive professional sports in protest? Ask the students what would be some alternatives to professional sports attendance. Perhaps Zirin and others could start supporting minor leagues or their local teams, or they could look to less expensive professional sports. For example, in the United States, professional soccer is not as expensive as American football. Parents could also focus on attending their children's events or even start participating in sports themselves. Teens and young adults could attend their friend's events or join a team. Zirin does not introduce these possibilities. Why not? Ask students how these alternatives might affect Zirin's argument. Would they be distracting, or can they coexist?

Perhaps one reason professional sports have such a powerful following is precisely *because* people have stopped playing sports themselves. So, they live vicariously through the players, often getting fat on the couch and drinking beer. Another way of reacting to the increase in ticket prices is to find other alternatives. What other alternatives can students propose? How could this rise in ticket prices stimulate positive change? How would looking for positive solutions affect Zirin's argument?

Thinking Critically about This Reading

Owners of franchises have to attract the best players, and for better or for worse salary motivates players' decisions. Owners also have to invest a great deal of money promoting their team. Between the cost of the players, promotion, perhaps increasing costs of stadium maintenance and investment (digital boards, nice seats, and so forth), the cost of transporting the team in first class, and lobbying with local governments for zoning and traffic influx, owners have lots of costs to cover. They are responsible for crowd management, too. Professional sports are also professional performances. They often have fancy half-time shows with stars who insist on large payments for their time. Big productions have big costs, and although many sports owners are independently wealthy, they most likely do not make the bulk of their wealth from their sports franchise.

Questions for Study and Discussion

1. Zirin's thesis is in paragraph 9: "Owners are uniquely charged with being the stewards of the game. It's a task that they have failed to perform in spectacular fashion." Zirin has presented a variety of evidence that the owners

have turned away from their originally supportive fans and have changed the experience for the fans. He cites the extra TV commercials (4), the increase in ticket prices (4), and the price of a beer (23). In paragraphs 10 and 21, he presents the existence of public funds as evidence that the fans are owed something, because they are in effect paying for the stadiums.

2. Zirin paints the picture of a likable coach, whom he'll use as a contrast to today's owners. The coach was a real guy, not perfect, but loved. Zirin implies that the hammer metaphor presented by the coach could also apply to professional sports. Today's owners have misused the "hammer," hitting fans on the head, rather than serving them.

3. Student opinions will vary. Zirin's short paragraphs speed up the essay, making it move quickly like a sports game. They also allow him to make powerful statements that stand out. "Sports fans are fed up" (3), for example, stands out and also gives the essay a dialogue feel, as if Zirin is giving a speech, participating in a debate, or responding to an interview.

4. Lupica seems to believe that sports are about the game itself, not the fans. Zirin responds to this point by arguing that the presence of public funds to support the teams makes the owners accountable to the public.

5. Zirin uses figurative language in paragraph 1 when he says that his couch "could spit tobacco hard enough to break a window." In paragraph 2, he uses figurative language to describe the change in professional sports: "If sports was once like a playful puppy you would wrestle on the floor, it's now like a housecat demanding to be stroked and giving nothing in return." In paragraph 10, he says the old paternalistic team owner is "as outdated as the typewriter."

Classroom Activity Using Argument

In debate, it is often helpful to have a timekeeper. Each side ought to have 5 minutes to present its argument, then 2 to 3 minutes for rebuttal, and finally a closing statement from each side. This structure moves the debate along quickly and also teaches students to respond quickly with thoughtful comments. You may also want to ask the students to vote at the end of the debate on which team was stronger and discuss why.

In Praise of the F Word (p. 564)
■ **Mary Sherry**

Essay Analysis and Discussion

Anything that involves short-term sacrifice to achieve long-term benefits is hard to sell in our society, and Mary Sherry knows it. But she also knows that her perspective as an adult literacy teacher carries weight when it comes to addressing those who would argue that failing is too traumatic for kids. In particular, notice how she organizes paragraphs 2 through 4. She begins by saying what she does, she progresses to what she has learned about her school and what difficulties students and teachers there face, and only at the end of paragraph 4 does she bring up the word "failure." By the time she gets to that word, she has established her experience and credibility. She has also implied that the schools have, in some cases, failed their students by not being willing to fail them. Also notice how paragraphs 10 through 12 make up what is essentially a three-paragraph conclusion. Much of the text in the three paragraphs would be repetitive and unnecessary if Sherry believed that she were addressing sympathetic readers, but it is clear that she believes that it is important to drive her point home. Discuss these and other techniques Sherry uses to persuade her presumably reluctant audience.

Thinking Critically about This Reading

By providing students with the opportunity to fail, teachers are enabling students to show that they can succeed. If students always pass, no matter how poor their work, success is devalued. Students may disagree with Sherry's statement.

Questions for Study and Discussion

1. Sherry's thesis is that flunking kids—or even the possibility of flunking them—can motivate many of them in the short term and prevent many long-term problems. She uses her experience as both an adult literacy program teacher and a parent as evidence.

2. Sherry acknowledges the opposition to flunking in paragraphs 8 and 11, but her strong language—*cheats* and *excuses*—clearly shows how she thinks. She does not detail the reasons—mostly economic and social—for a policy of passing students, probably because she believes that such a discussion would get her argument off track by focusing on issues other than the students themselves. Sherry's experiences with students in her adult literacy program who have been "passed along" without mastering basic materials while in school argue strongly for a system that gets "tough" with students and encourages them with the threat of failure to make school a priority.

3. The "F word" can mean either failure or flunking. By calling it the "F word," Sherry implies that it has now become a taboo concept to flunk kids.

4. Sherry's audience is presumably educators and parents. They do not appear to be receptive to the "F word." Students should note the gradual introduction of the concept of failure, the long conclusion, and the personal examples.

5. Sherry has seen the results of passing marginally literate and illiterate students—severe problems after graduation and a need to go back to school. The second part is a matter of personal opinion.

The reliability of evidence is, of course, what drives writers, scholars, doctors, lawyers, and researchers to do what they do. Finding more than one authority who agrees with the assumption of the reliability of a body of evidence some-times can make a case for accuracy, but sometimes such reliance only proves that scholars rely too heavily on the unexamined and untested work of their predecessors. A writer we know, for example, has been working on a book on the covered bridges of Vermont. Finding some discrepancies in the measure-ments of those bridges in source materials, he thought it necessary to take his own measurements. He found that not only were early published statistics inaccurate, but subsequent researchers and writers had relied on that informa-tion and republished it. The issue of reliability often raises the question of how much time a writer or other professional has to accomplish a given task. It should be made clear, however, that writing based on questionable informa-tion may so distort the conclusions that the whole endeavor becomes a waste of time.

Crime: What Constitutes an Effective Punishment?

Condemn the Crime, Not the Person (p. 569)
■ June Tangney

Essay Analysis and Discussion

One of the distinctions between Tangney's and Kahan's essays is that Tangney distinguishes between shame and guilt. She claims that each has "very different implications for subsequent moral and interpersonal behavior" (paragraph 5). You may have an interesting discussion by asking students whether they agree with Tangney about the difference between guilt and shame. Is the difference more in the consequence than in the punishment?

Thinking Critically about This Reading

Tangney cites "recent scientific evidence" (4) that shows that those who receive shaming sentences have the same outcomes as those who receive standard prison sentences. Public shaming and stigmatization are counterproductive. Al-though they may satisfy the public's thirst for brute and open punishments, they neither deter crimes nor prevent recidivism.

Questions for Study and Discussion

1. Shaming sentences are "sanctions explicitly designed to induce feelings of shame" (1). Judges choose these sentences over more traditional ones be-

cause the cost of incarceration remains high and the success rate extremely low. The judges believe that they need alternatives.

2. Tangney believes that shame causes more harm than good. She believes that there is a strong and important difference between shame and guilt, and that they lead to different behaviors and outcomes. Shame actually makes a bad situation worse by diminishing the person's sense of self and does not encourage better behavior. Guilt focuses on the bad behavior—not the bad person—and therefore encourages reparative action.

3. According to Tangney, "recent scientific evidence suggests that such attempts at social control are misguided. Rather than fostering constructive change, shame often makes a bad situation worse" (4).

4. Tangney answers the rhetorical question by stating, "Well, one way is to force offenders to focus on the negative consequences of their behavior, particularly on the painful negative consequences for others" (13). Students may also suggest asking offenders to think of a punishment themselves or asking the victims of the crime to suggest a punishment. Others may suggest educating the offenders on the effects of their actions.

5. Tangney says that other methods prove ineffective and perhaps destructive, that "thoughtfully constructed guilt-oriented community service sentences are more likely to foster changes in offenders' future behaviors, while contributing to the larger societal good" (18). She thinks that any good community volunteer would welcome this positive outcome and not take it as an insult to his or her work.

Classroom Activity Using Argument

Audience is an abstraction for most writers. They have a vague sense of why it might be more helpful to say this or that, with such and such diction, but they don't really study the issue, the importance of not missing the target at every point in the writing. We find this exercise helpful in getting students to think more practically about the audience for their work. Types of evidence students should consider include the following:

1. A lot of basic information is conveyed if the audience is deemed by the writer to be uninformed on the subject.

2. Key terms and concepts are defined if the audience is uninformed.

3. Technical language is used if the audience is presumed to be familiar with the subject.

4. Unexamined assumptions that would not pass muster with less friendly readers would be offered if the audience is like-minded or sympathetic.

Shame Is Worth a Try (p. 574)
■ Dan M. Kahan

Essay Analysis and Discussion

Kahan makes an economic argument for the use of shaming punishments in place of imprisonment for minor crimes. Shaming punishments are cheaper to carry out than incarceration, and they also allow convicts to contribute to the economy by making restitution to their victims or making child-support payments, for example.

Thinking Critically about This Reading

Kahan's argument is based on the economics of punishment for minor crimes — shaming punishments are as effective as prison sentences but vastly less expensive. Combining traditional sentences *and* shaming punishments, as in the case of sex offenders, negates the economic benefit of shaming sentences alone.

Questions for Study and Discussion

1. Kahan's thesis is stated in paragraph 3: "[W]hat the shame proponents seem to be getting, and the critics ignoring, is the potential of shame as an effective, cheap, and humane alternative to imprisonment."

2. "Steal from your employer in Wisconsin and you might be ordered to wear a sandwich board proclaiming your offense. Drive drunk in Florida or Texas and you might be required to place a conspicuous 'DUI' bumper sticker to your car. Refuse to make your child-support payments in Virginia and you will find that your vehicle has been immobilized with an appropriately colored boot (pink if the abandoned child is a girl, blue if it is a boy)" (1). Student opinions will differ regarding the question of the appropriateness of such punishments.

3. Kahan sees imprisonment as crueler than shame. In one sense, shame is less cruel for both the individual and society because it enables offenders to continue earning an income, compensating the victim, paying child support, and contributing to society. In paragraph 11, he states that "shame clearly doesn't hurt as much as imprisonment. Individuals who go to jail end up just as disgraced as those who are shamed."

4. Kahan cites a series of studies by Harold Grasmick suggesting that "the prospect of public disgrace exerts greater pressure to comply with the law than does the threat of imprisonment and other formal punishments" (9).

5. Students will have different reactions to Kahan's argument. Some might say that they would like to hear about some experiences from the offenders themselves. Did shaming work in Wisconsin? Students may raise the question, not addressed by Kahan, "Will shame be more effective for some

126

people than for others?" Others may agree with Kahan that shaming punishments are worth a try.

6. Kahan's argument in favor of trying shame as a punishment is worthwhile. Its chief strength is its economic benefit. It costs less than incarceration. Its weakness as an argument is that shame may be subject to abuse (then again all punishment is prone to abuse), and it may also not work with certain crimes such as "requiring sex offenders to register with local authorities." We do not want to save money by putting the public in harm's way.

Classroom Activity Using Argument

A variation on this activity would be to focus specifically on the potential harm of violent content in entertainment. Assuming your classroom is technologically equipped for it, debaters can use examples from their own cultural milieu to illustrate their points.

Petty Crime, Outrageous Punishment (p. 579)
■ Carl M. Cannon

Essay Analysis and Discussion

Who determines how severe a punishment a "crime" or indiscretion deserves? When we are children, parents and teachers decide, and there is no independent tribunal to consider if their punishments are just. Ask students if they remember punishments that they thought were unjust growing up. For example, did they lie about doing their homework and were not allowed to go to a friend's birthday party? The content of this essay raises these important questions. How do we know what is unjust and when there is injustice, and who speaks up for those who cannot speak for themselves? In a sense, children are similar to criminals in that they can rarely challenge decisions of those in authority all by themselves. The importance of Cannon's essay is that he has chosen to defend those with less freedom to speak. Discuss with students the importance of being able to make a good argument, especially when people's lives are at stake. This essay argues for action and change that can deeply affect people's lives. Discuss with students the importance of being able to argue well—not just to do well on academic papers written in college and to impress teachers, but because our ability to make a case articulately with *ethos, pathos,* and *logos* could change lives.

Thinking Critically about This Reading

You also may want to widen this discussion in class to address the many countries in the world that do not adhere to this same philosophy. China, for example, has a legal system that favors order over individual rights. Societies that favor order over justice will imprison many people with all sorts of harsh penalties. In these countries, advocating for these prisoners is almost impossible.

Questions for Study and Discussion

1. Cannon states his thesis in paragraph 4; many people are serving extremely long sentences for low-level crimes as "the result of well-intentioned anti-crime laws that have gone terribly wrong."

2. In paragraph 22, he starts making some recommendations. He states that "the law needs to be more flexible than some rigid slogan." In paragraph 29, he speaks out against mandatory minimums.

3. Cannon uses *cause and effect* in paragraphs 5 and 6. He talks about how the mandatory minimums implemented in the 1990s have caused a "fall-out." The result has been that thousands of people who were convicted of petty crimes serve unusually harsh sentences. He makes this point using narration. He *narrates* Andrade's story to make his point. Andrade stole videos and received a penalty harsher than many receive for manslaughter or sexual assault. Cannon uses *illustration* in paragraphs 11 and 12. To illustrate that he knows the benefits of harsh penalties, he cites the decreasing crime rates in California and Florida after tough sentencing was implemented.

4. This information increases the reader's empathy for Andrade. How could you punish a man so harshly for stealing sweet cartoons for his children? They are the kinds of details a defense attorney would mention to the jury to illicit empathy and compassion for the client. In addition, they also make the reader consider that the movies were perhaps really for Andrade's kids and not just to sell for drugs. If they were movies to sell for drug money, would they have been kids' movies? Maybe, maybe not.

5. Student opinions will vary. Some students may believe that citations would have given the essay a more academic tone and been off-putting for that reason. Others may argue that the citations would elevate his essay for just the same reason. They might feel more confident reusing his examples when discussing the topic with others if they knew that they were documented instead of potential urban myths. If the author is proved wrong, it could hurt his credibility in future articles as well as his ability to receive writing assignments.

6. In paragraph 7, the reference to the titles of the DVDs is a tonal lapse. The contrast is so striking between the seriousness of the penalty compared to the innocence of these films. In paragraph 13, he uses slang in a way that constitutes a tonal lapse: "For a state with a battered economy, that's a pile of money to spend on sweeping up petty crooks." He uses a similar tonal switch at the end of paragraph 22, when he says, "Well, that's hard to figure out." In a sense, he introduces a sarcastic tone that clearly distinguishes

the essay as a more informal *Reader's Digest* one versus an article destined for academic publication.

Classroom Activity Using Argument

1. America: Love it or leave it! *Either/or thinking*
2. Two of my best friends who are overweight don't exercise at all. Overweight people are simply not getting enough exercise. *Hasty overgeneralization*
3. If we use less gasoline, the price of gasoline will fall. *Oversimplification*
4. Life is precious because we want to protect it at all costs. *False analogy*
5. Randy is a good mechanic, so he'll be a good racecar driver. *Non sequitur*
6. Susan drank hot lemonade, and her cold went away. *Post hoc, ergo propter hoc*
7. Students do poorly in college because they do too much surfing on the Web. *Begging the question*
8. If we can eliminate pollution, we can cure cancer. *Oversimplification*
9. Such actions are illegal because they are prohibited by law. *Begging the question*
10. Every time I have something important to do on my computer, it crashes. *Post hoc, ergo propter hoc*
11. We should either raise taxes or cut social programs. *Either/or thinking*
12. Education ought to be managed just as a good business is managed. *False analogy*

Advertising: How Does It Affect Our Lives?

The Piracy of Privacy (p. 587)
■ Allen D. Kanner

Essay Analysis and Discussion

This essay focuses on the negatives of increasing brand knowledge of our activities. Discuss with your students the counterargument. What are some of the benefits, if any, of these and upcoming advances? For example, it arguably could be helpful and pleasant for Nike to send a coupon once you have run the recommended number of miles in your shoes and now need to replace them. Or, perhaps stores know what you bought last week and have some shoe suggestions that would match. In some ways, the brands could do the work for you and you would just relax, set your preferences, and let them find you. Perhaps we would spend less time hunting for items and clipping coupons.

Thinking Critically about This Reading

Kanner uses mostly inductive reasoning. He builds up points leading to his conclusion. He provides many specific instances where privacy is being challenged and uses that to conclude in his penultimate paragraph that "the damage wrought is an inevitable byproduct of the economic system" (17).

Questions for Study and Discussion

1. Kanner states his thesis in paragraph 1: "Corporate advertising constitutes the greatest threat to privacy in human history."
2. Kanner's purpose is to demonstrate to the reader the different ways brands are invading privacy. He wants us to create alternative economic models that do not lead to such an invasion of privacy.
3. Kanner provides a variety of evidence that our privacy has been breached. GPS in smartphones track individuals' movement and offer them coupons based on their location (4), some digital billboard companies have a digital camera that gathers information on passersby (6), web portals gather huge amounts of data on web customers (7), new research in neuromarketing promises to make advertising more effective—going deeper into our brains (9), and the increasing integration of our devices means more opportunities for advertisers to gather information and cross promote (10).
4. In his last paragraph (18), he says that the answer is not regulation. He believes that it will not be significant enough to protect us in the long term. He wants to change the game altogether.
5. *Ethos:* Kanner argues for privacy, a topic he conveys as vital to all readers. He establishes credibility by providing myriad concrete examples, described in answer 3, that demonstrate how this invasion is occurring. Kanner successfully organizes and presents his examples. His ability to be specific helps both *ethos* and *logos*. He is able to name specific companies, brands, and amounts and kinds of data being processed. In terms of *pathos,* Kanner refers to companies and brands that will be familiar to most readers. In doing so, he maintains connection with his readers. He also, in paragraphs 11–13, outlines a hypothetical future situation that reaches readers in a different tone. He helps them imagine how it might affect their future and the future of their children. This combination of personal with the professional makes up Kanner's *pathos.*
6. Kanner wants to reach people who are like-minded or potentially like-minded. Had he wanted to reach people who were pro-advertising, he most likely would have presented and responded to counterarguments, which he does not do.

Classroom Activity Using Argument

1. The validity of Kanner's findings can be confirmed through some Internet searching.
2. Consumers could refuse to have information shared by searching for or creating a service that allows people to benefit from technology without the invasion of privacy. For example, someone could start a smartphone com-

pany that guarantees that no information will be shared. Kanner would like the consumer to help develop a new economic model. Ask students how could one do that.

3. Corporations and media research companies can only do media research on those who "opt-in" to the study. For more than 40 years, 90 percent of media research has been done with people who agree to answer questions about brand usage or who agree to carry a device that measures their media consumption.

4. If life is about creation or survival, American business "is" life. If life were about "privacy," business would be antilife. It depends on what you think life is about. Ask students to describe what life is to them. Thinking about this question and topic will help them then determine if American business is antilife.

Marketing Ate Our Culture—But It Doesn't Have To (p. 594)
■ Terry O'Reilly

Essay Analysis and Discussion

O'Reilly's defense of advertising is especially powerful because he begins by voicing the opinions of those who have argued against it. Starting out with a counterargument increases his credibility with readers, because it shows the essay's audience that O'Reilly has considered other perspectives. O'Reilly's argument for advertising is based around the notion of a "great unwritten contract" between advertiser and consumer. You may want to ask students to compare this argument with that of Dave Zirin in his essay "What Pro Sports Owners Owe Us." Zirin also uses the argument that a contract exists that one party has breached. In Zirin's article, he refers to the agreement between the team's owner and the fans. Ask students to discuss these unwritten social contracts and to find other examples of unwritten agreements between people that others break. Etiquette is a social contract. Even parking lots have etiquette that not everyone follows. For example, if you are waiting behind a car that is exiting, you have priority over a new car arriving from the other direction. This priority is not a law, but a social contract. Essays such as Zirin's and O'Reilly's use the notion of breach of contract to frame their arguments. Do students think that these contracts really exist and imply moral obligations, or are they just creations used to support one's personal preferences?

Thinking Critically about This Reading

1. O'Reilly states his thesis in the first paragraph: "You might just have a moral obligation to watch more commercials."

2. In paragraph 2, he uses narration when telling the story of Claudia Alta Taylor Johnson inspiring her husband and the U.S. president to place limits on the billboards in Texas. He uses narration again in paragraph 5 when he sticks a "bookmark" and goes back in time. The bookmark leads into the equivalent of a flashback, a tool of narration. This flashback includes a narration reviewing the history of Lasker's and Aylesworth's response to the new medium of radio advertising. O'Reilly uses these narrations to demonstrate the origins of the social contract that he claims exists between advertisers and consumers. He claims that the contract existed for decades and was upheld by both sides until recently.

3. O'Reilly uses analogies in paragraph 9 when he offers the readers examples of other compromises and draws the advertising/advertiser analogy to that of camping and flying: "You want to go camping? You tolerate mosquitos. You want to fly? You tolerate removing your belt at airports." In paragraph 21, he equates the advertising contract with a marriage contract: "No one said marriage was easy." In paragraph 26, he goes on to equate the skipping of ads with a roofer or dentist not completing his or her work: "If a roofing contractor took your money, and didn't replace your roof, you'd be outraged. If your dentist sent you a bill but didn't fill the cavity, you'd bounce off all four walls."

4. O'Reilly uses the bookmark like a flashback device. He is able to hold his argument in place while going back in time to give the discussion some historical context. He returns to bookmark in paragraph 13, to tie the past into the present. His point was that even advertising greats like Ogilvy agree that there is a social contract. The bookmark device allows O'Reilly to take a historical detour without losing his reader.

5. O'Reilly uses the point about "mass audience" for radio to make the case that radio provided a special shared experience for thousands of people. Radio gave something valuable to the culture, he believes, and he argues that a quick sponsorship message was a small price to pay for such benefits.

6. The Great Unwritten Contract is that advertising must give you something back in exchange for the time it takes away. It must be relevant, be clever, or provide something of value; and because it sponsors our favorite shows, in exchange the consumer must watch the ad. Students may or may not agree that such an unwritten contract exists.

7. O'Reilly's article is primarily written for people who avoid ads by leaving the room, deleting them, or changing the channel to avoid them. He wants his audience to watch the ads presented during the programs.

Classroom Activity Using Argument

You may want to ask students what they think of billboards that are mounted in ugly neighborhoods or highways. Not all billboards are posted on highways with beautiful scenery. There are billboards leaving San Francisco on the Bay

Bridge that arguably improve the landscape as well as billboards after you have crossed the East River towards Yankee Stadium. Billboards can be a pleasant alternative to landscapes filled with concrete buildings and factories. You also may want to discuss with students how and why outdoor advertising has increased in recent years. Because people cannot delete the ads, change the channel, or click them away, outdoor advertising maintains a special appeal among advertisers. Outdoor advertising is also not just limited to billboards; it includes everything from pizza boxes to bus shelters, digital signage, laundry bags, malls, and more. Ask students if they feel the same about these means of outdoor advertising. Are they better or worse than billboards?

Generation E. A.: Ethnically Ambiguous (p. 602)
■ **Ruth La Ferla**

Essay Analysis and Discussion

The mosaic concept is not really discussed in this essay, although questions relate to this section. You may want to have the general discussion about the difference between mosaic and melting pot before discussing the essay. Each generation searches for a way to be distinct. Students may have deep feelings about these issues, deeper than they may consciously know. Consider a 5-minute free write on whether they would want to live in a mosaic or a melting pot and why.

Thinking Critically about This Reading

The melting pot is the idea that all ethnic groups of people merge and combine to become one group. The differences melt away, and one culture is formed. The mosaic idea is that each individual or group retains his or her distinctive attributes and lives in harmony next to others with their own attributes. The melting pot emphasizes change and the mosaic acceptance.

Questions for Study and Discussion

1. Her thesis is stated most clearly in paragraph 5: "Ambiguity is chic, especially among the under-25 members of Generation Y, the most racially diverse population in the nation's history." Students might claim that the thesis is in paragraph 2: "It is also a look that is reflected in the latest youth marketing trend: using faces that are ethnically ambiguous." Either view could be correct in terms of where the thesis is stated most clearly.
2. She uses evidence that the ethnically ambiguous Mr. Jimenez has been the choice of Levi's, DKNY, and Aldo. Louis Vuitton, YSL Beauty, and H&M have also highlighted similarly ambiguous models. She also cites the popularity of such figures as Lisa Bonet and Jessica Alba.

3. In the 2000 census, "nearly seven million Americans identified themselves as members of more than once race" (7). She uses this statistic as evidence that the ethnic makeup of the country is evolving.

4. Students may say that the trend indicates the nation is moving more toward the melting pot concept and away from the mosaic concept. All the different groups are melting together. This melding could lead either to an increase or a decrease of the traditions of the groups. If the generation is interested in the traditions of each part, they may seek to retain them. If not, a new culture will be formed.

5. As people start to identify themselves as belonging to more than one ethnic group, ambiguity will increase and the culture will change.

6. Life is now ethnically ambiguous, so the art of modeling and fashion photography now have to keep up with that reality. As expressed in a common expression, "life imitates art." For example, people will try to live the lives they see on TV. Now, however, TV has to mimic instead of lead.

Classroom Activity Using Argument

Guzzardi challenges La Ferla's argument that the United States is becoming rapidly more ethnically ambiguous. He quotes statistics from UPI national correspondent Steve Sailer, who notes the following:

- Only 3.5 percent of married non-Hispanic whites intermarry.
- Only 6 percent of black husbands and 2 percent of black wives are in interracial marriages.
- Slightly less than 18 percent of Hispanic wives have non-Hispanic husbands, while slightly more than 15 percent of Hispanic husbands have non-Hispanic wives.
- About 18 percent of Asian wives have white husbands, but only 7 percent of Asian husbands have white wives.
- Sailer also noted that immigrants are least likely to marry outside of their group.

Torture: Are We For or Against It?

The Truth about Torture (p. 616)
■ **Charles Krauthammer**

Essay Analysis and Discussion

Krauthammer frames his argument in reference to McCain's position. In paragraph 2, he says that McCain's position deserves respect. Debates, written or verbal, can be a bit like the beginning of a fighting match. In most martial arts, the opponents bow and then proceed to attack each other. Ask students to consider how Krauthammer's acknowledgment of McCain is a bit like a bow before the fight. How does honoring the opponent help Krauthammer gain the respect of his own readers? Consider together some other ways a writer can acknowledge the other side. For example, the writer can say where his or her opponent has been correct or demonstrate an understanding of the origin of the other side's opinion. This discussion of other views can also serve to organize the essay. In the end, Krauthammer claims that his and McCain's positions are not really that far from one another, using a collaborative debating technique.

Thinking Critically about This Reading

Given his particular personal experience with torture, one might assume that McCain would be more skeptical of the method than he seems to be. This question asks students to consider whether or not personal experience, in this case, has fragmented McCain's political stance on the issue instead of solidified it.

Questions for Study and Discussion

1. Krauthammer's thesis is most clearly described in paragraph 13, although some students might cite earlier statements. In paragraph 13, he says, "However rare the cases, there are circumstances in which, by any rational moral calculus, torture not only would be permissible but would be required (to acquire life saving information)."

2. Krauthammer's purpose in writing this essay is to clarify when torture makes sense, to show that he and McCain are ultimately on the same side, and to argue that no amendment is needed.

3. In paragraphs 3 through 9, Krauthammer classifies three types of war prisoners. He makes this classification to show the reader that he has carefully considered when torture is necessary as well as to demonstrate that he does support the rights of prisoners in many cases and that torture would only apply to particular kinds of prisoners. In making this distinction, he helps readers understand that he is not someone looking to punish anyone who is not on his side. These distinctions are also designed to demonstrate that one can be rational and moral even in the context of torture. Students might find other purposes that this classification serves.

4. Khalid Sheik Mohammed, a Pakistani (later a Bosnian), was charged in 2008 with war crimes and murder. He is in the custody of the United States at Guantanamo Bay. He was a member of al-Qaeda and is considered the "principle architect" of the September 11, 2001, attacks. He underwent waterboarding. Krauthammer uses him because he believes that Khalid Sheik Mohammed is a good example of someone who deserves to suffer, describing him as a "murderer of 2,973 innocents, is surely deserving of the most extreme suffering day and night for the rest of his life" (33). He is also an example of someone, had he been captured and tortured prior to the plan, may have provided information necessary to avert the disaster.

5.   In paragraph 39, Krauthammer demonstrates why he thinks that the Mc-Cain argument is for show. He says that McCain is stated as saying that, under certain circumstances, he could disobey the very amendment for which he advocates. Student opinions will vary.

6.   Student opinions will vary. If students are against torture at all costs, along the lines of Sullivan's essay, "The Abolition of Torture," which follows Krauthammer's essay in the text, they will most likely argue for a shorter essay. Why keep discussing it if it is a moot point? On the other hand, if students are considering Krauthammer's arguments or agree fundamentally, they will find his multiple distinctions to be useful. In torture, perhaps, the devil is in the details.

Classroom Activity Using Argument

1.   Post hoc, ergo propter hoc
2.   Non sequitur
3.   Oversimplification
4.   False analogy
5.   Begging the question

The Abolition of Torture (p. 629)
■ **Andrew Sullivan**

Essay Analysis and Discussion

Sullivan argues a clear position: Any torture is a betrayal of our values. Discuss the benefits of taking a side versus arguing for the middle position. Although the middle position may be more realistic in any debate, arguing a decisive side has its advantages when writing. Ask students why committing to a perspective can be easier for writers than arguing for the middle position. When taking a middle position, writers must leave the argument/counterargument structure. They must represent the extremes and argue for the middle. Ask students how a middle position essay on this topic could be structured.

Thinking Critically about This Reading

Fishman's statement that "if we abandon our ideals in the face of adversity and aggression, then those ideas were never really in our possession" (paragraph 31) summarizes his overarching feeling about this topic. He believes that for our ideals of personal liberty and for the rights of man truly to be ours, we cannot betray them in any circumstances. With regard to torture, this stance means that if, under any circumstances, we implement methods of torture to achieve any goal, we are, in a sense, saying that we never truly valued the rights of man. For Fishman, any betrayal is a total denial. For students, it might be interesting to introduce the concept in other, softer circumstances. For example, does smoking socially only on occasion suggest that a smoker really never quit smoking? How much does one need to smoke to be a "smoker"? How much does one need to torture to be a torturer?

Questions for Study and Discussion

1. Sullivan states his thesis in paragraph 3 when he says that "torture, in any form and under any circumstances, is both antithetical to the most basic principles for which the United States stands and a profound impediment to winning a wider war that we cannot afford to lose."

2. Sullivan responds to Krauthammer's practical points saying, first, that any acts of torture must be the exception and that those involved must be accountable to the law and, second, that the danger of permitting torture in any case allows it to spread. In paragraph 19, he summarizes his arguments as suggesting "our 'dirty hands' be wiped legally clean before and after the fact." Sullivan believes that if there are isolated cases when one must break the rule, there ought to be consequences, just as there are when anyone breaks a rule. He believes that being a free country means being accountable for breaking laws. He also argues importantly in paragraph 20 that "once you permit torture for someone somewhere, it has a habit of spreading." Student opinions will vary regarding the effectiveness of these counterarguments.

3. The debate is emotional because it is about people's lives and suffering relative to our own needs for national security. It does not mean that the debate is without logos or ethos. It pitches our deepest primal fears against our sense of what is right or moral. People have an innate sense, if not an experiential one, of how soul-crushing torture can be. Anyone with any sense of compassion or empathy inevitably feels moved by this debate.

4. In paragraph 13, Sullivan attempts to convince the reader that his desire to defeat terrorism is as strong or stronger than anyone else's: "Let me state for the record that I am second to none in decrying, loathing, and desiring to defeat those who wish to replace freedom with religious tyranny of the most brutal kind." This statement may convince some students that Sullivan is *not* soft on terrorism. Others, however, might believe that his position on torture makes him soft regardless of his rhetoric to the contrary.

5. Sullivan defines *torture* in paragraph 2 and *break* in paragraph 5. The definition of torture is critical because the debate cannot begin until we agree upon terms. If one person thinks that imprisonment is torture and another defines it as waterboarding, no meaningful discussion can be had. Definition of terms is one of the most commonly used tools in debate. *Break* has to be defined for two reasons. First, Sullivan wants to distinguish between the breaking of a nose, for example, and the breaking of a soul. Second, in defining the term, he highlights the depth of what is happening during the

137

process. More than just enduring physical pain, a person finds himself or herself crushed into what he calls "something subhuman" (5). Definition provides Sullivan a tool to bring the reader closer to the details of what we are talking about. Krauthammer speaks in more general terms that help him make his point.

6. Sullivan begins with a question, which can often be a powerful way to hook the reader. In the ending, he answers that question of, "why is torture wrong" (1), with his answer: "If we legalize torture, even under constrained conditions, we will have given up a large part of the idea that is America. We have lost the war before we have given ourselves the chance to win it" (31).

Classroom Activity Using Argument

1. False analogy
2. Oversimplification
3. Hasty generalization
4. Non sequitur
5. Post hoc, ergo propter hoc